MW01505365

GARDENING BY MYSELF.

Photo by W. H. Stockbridge

ANNA B. WARNER

GARDENING BY MYSELF.

BY

ANNA WARNER.

Nor does he govern only, or direct,
But much performs himself.
THE TASK.

Published in cooperation with
THE CONSTITUTION ISLAND ASSOCIATION

APPLEWOOD BOOKS
Bedford, Massachusetts

Gardening by Myself was first published in 1872 by
Anson D. F. Randolph & Co. of New York City. The
book was set into type by Edward O. Jenkins, printer
and stereotyper, also of New York.

Thank you for purchasing an Applewood Book.
Applewood reprints America's lively classics—books
from the past that are still of interest to modern readers.
For a free copy of our current catalog, write to
Applewood Books, P.O. Box 365, Bedford, MA 01730.

10 9 8 7 6 5 4 3 2 1

This facsimile of the original
1872 edition of "Gardening by Myself"
is dedicated to

BLAIR HAWES DAVIES

Master Gardener and lifelong friend
of the Constitution Island Association

Constitution Island Association, Inc.
Box 41, West Point, NY 10996
Tel: (845)446-8676   Fax: (845)622-6022

The Constitution Island Association, Inc.
is a 501(c)(3) non-profit organization.
All contributions are tax deductible.
Member contributions have maintained
the Warner House for almost 90 years.
Tours are scheduled
from May through September.
Please visit us online at
www.constitutionisland.org.

CONTENTS

_____

Preface

January 5

February 23

March 38

April 54

May 70

June 92

July 117

August 148

September 163

October 182

November 201

December 214

ILLUSTRATIONS

Anna B. Warner......................*Frontispiece*

PAGE

Hanging-Basket of Cocoa-Nut Shell, with Kenilworth Ivy 5

Maple Seed Cut to Shew the Folded Plant }
Plant Taken Out } ... 25

Maple, with Seed Leaves Unfolded }
Maple, Shewing the First Pair of Leaves } 26

Set of Ladies's Garden Tools.................. 40

Ladies's Wheelbarrow 42

Section of Maple Root to Show the Cells........ 56

Morning Glory in Seed-leaf.................... 74

Morning Glory with First Leaves Out.......... 75

Home-Made Hand Glass 78

Stick and String Supports.................... 89

Miss Warner's House and Part of Her Garden.. 94

Pot Frame 103

Frame for Roses, etc. 104

Short Pruning. Slant Pruning 106

Vine Support 111

Layer, Showing Cut, Peg, Wedge, etc. 129

Prepared Bud 131

Stock with Incisions. Stock with Bud Inserted.. 132

Stock and Bud Bound Up 133

Cutting as Set Out.......................... 138

Cutting as Set Out........................... 139

Moss Basket 143

Rustic Box 144

Dahlia Rings 148

PREFACE.

GARDENING by oneself is so lovely, and so easy a thing, that I would fain have everybody try it. Do not mistake me: you cannot do *everything* without glass and gardeners, and that convenient helper popularly called "The Bank of England." But you can do so much, that you may well be content; and even be able to listen quietly to some one giving an unlimited order for priceless carnations, what though the thought comes to you (as it did to me):

"I had but three, my own seedlings, and a grub eat up one of them."

The thought that there are two left, will be very sweet to you, even then and there Touchwood's label is not the worst that can be put upon a plant:

"A poor thing, sir, but mine own."

But there is no need of raising poor things; and you can hardly imagine, beforehand, how much dearer such friend-flowers are, than any, even the most splendid, mere acquaintances introduced by a professed gardener.

I wish everybody had a garden, and would work in it himself,—the world would grow sweeter-tempered at once. Why you may deal with one great florist after another, (I know, for I have dealt with a good many) and you will find nothing but courtesy and pleasant words from the beginning to the end. No urging you to take what you do not want, no clipping the measure of what you buy; but on the contrary, your insignificant little orders are rounded out with unexpected treasures. As if the florists could not bear even to think of empty gardens, while theirs were so full; or else had a sort of gentle sympathy for the people who expect to live upon fifty cents' worth of flowers for a whole year.

I think it is Mr. Biglow who solaces himself with " More last words." I know there are many I might say. There are flower names you will look for here, and not find. The fair faces of my Campanula Lorei, look at me reproachfully even now, from a distance; with the pink Eucharidiums, just unfolding their fresh colour. And there is Viola Cornuta, and my superb new *Gen. Jacqueminot* rose. But if I mentioned everything, when should I have done? Not till my book was altogether too big for you to buy.   SHAHWEETAH, *June 28*, 1872.

GARDENING BY MYSELF.

JANUARY.

Pines, ef you're blue, are the best friends I know,
They mope an' sigh an' sheer your feelin's so.

—Lowell.

I THINK it is not common to choose this month for a visit to Fairyland. Yet, as you never do thoroughly know people unless you have lived with them, so neither do you well appreciate Fairyland, unless you have dwelt there all the year. All parts of it indeed are not open at all times; and just now an explorer

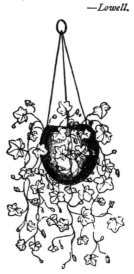

HANGING-BASKET OF COCOA-NUT SHELL, WITH KENILWORTH IVY.

must be content to tarry for awhile at the

1*

gates, making himself comfortable by the
lodge fire. But there are fair views to be
had from thence, and good reading is plenty, and abundant materials for consideration
and study ; and there is work enough to do,
if that's all, and if you know how to do it.
Oh ! but it is pleasant to escape into Fairyland from the every-day cares and labours
and dust, and to study the wonders God is
preparing, and to think of the underground
work in progress, and to use our own glad
hands as agents.   If they are glad and willing—that is enough; the skill will come.
And to help and encourage a wee bit, and
to advise just a little, I think I must tell
what Fairyland is to me.

I should say, to begin, that I do not mean
by this the enchanted regions of professed
gardeners, — neither of those people who
are blessed with that very useful, trouble-
some, self-willed appendage to a flower garden.   My Fairyland does not spring up
under glass, nor out of money, nor with
"facilities." For people having all these

I do not write,—nor for "young florists,"
intending to make the business their pro-
fession. Mr. Henderson's book may instruct
them.   *They* must begin all right, and work
on by line and rule.

But the people for whom I write begin
anywhere, — with the first flower or seed
they happen to pick up; and then work on—
anyhow ! That is, not heedlessly, nor neglect-
fully, but as they can. Therefore not by line
and rule, which is often an impossibility ; but
in some strange wildwood way making a
path through difficulties, and reaching their
Fairyland "cross lots." Well they know
what I mean, when I say that if you have
not a syringe you must water plants through
your fingers! Or if they do not, I can tell
them and they'll work it out.

With some people flowers are a fixed
fact, a necessity ; and thence follows endless
pains-taking, tireless patience, and wonderful success. They are the people for whom
"everything grows."

Do you see that old brown house by the

roadside?—guiltless of everything but weather paint?—and in the window an old rough box? Look now at the magnificent "lambrequin" of sweet peas, which drapes the window and almost hides the box in which they grow. There are no new varieties, it is true,—neither "striped, from Ceylon," nor scarlet, surnamed, "invincible." "Painted ladies," every one of them, but such a solid phalanx of their bonny faces I never saw.

Do you see this other house; low, unpretending? Two poor men live there—bachelor brothers; daily workers for their daily bread. There is no show of anything about the house, inside or out, with just one exception. Each side the front door, like a supporter of its humble dimensions, stands an immense hydrangea; with heads of bloom that can rival anything. And of the rare colour too (whichever that is !—I'm always as puzzled as the old woman about her bluing)—the colour that everybody tries for, and few can induce. All the other hydrangeas in the village are in their native

rose, but for the two old brothers the blossoms are always blue. (I know I'm right
now!) They have their secret, as to the
how and the why.

Next door to a small city church that I
have seen, stands the Sunday School house;
and in the third floor of this lives the sexton.
His little windows look down upon city
yards—poor specimens, some of them;—and
only the eastern lookout makes his windows
bright.

Across one of the windows, trained from
side to side till the whole is covered with a
net-work of twigs and leaves and blossoms,
a honeysuckle stretches its pretty sprays,
growing contentedly in a pot on that third
story window-sill. Or if not contentedly—
yet hiding its discontent in the most successful endeavors to brighten the small
world in which it lives. I said it was the
sexton's window—but I am quite sure the
honeysuckle belongs to his wife.

In a poorer home than this, in a tenement garret in London, stands an ivy; its

roots nourished in *four* flower-pots, its leaves curtaining the small windows, with their upper surface laid close against the glass. The old human inmate of the room " keeps herself happy by reading her Bible and loving her ivy !"—The plant and its poor owner seeking the light together, and finding it— even in a tenement house — with faces " pressed close to the glass."

Yes, for such people, " everything grows." Their loving skill—for I doubt if real love *can* long be ignorant—has a power of coaxing which finds its way to the very heart of a cutting, and makes seeds yield up their treasures with a precision and promptness quite distracting to ordinary mortals,—those easy, hopeful, blunderers who plant sweet peas on the top of the ground rather late, and petunias an inch deep, rather early ; and comfortably bestow all their failures at the seedman's door.

But real love has other skill than this; and can (somehow) draw gold-value from a purse of coppers, and fetch double-distilled

pleasure out of a solitary plant. Did ever
Mr. Vick's twenty acres of spring bloom
smell as sweet, I wonder, as a single fair little buff hyacinth that was given me long
ago? when it was my only one, and not even
the small amount of capital it represented
could have been spent by me for such a
luxury? Fairyland?—why that hyacinth
shone like Aladdin's palace, and was a new
surprise every time we looked at it.

Success will follow love. Didn't I beat
Mr. Vick with his own seed two years ago,
and raise green-edged petunias (P. margi-
nata) that were bigger " by a handful," as
the boys say, than the one he has put in his
new Chromo for 1871? But to begin:

January 1*st*,—and a bright clear day. No
snow on the ground, no fixed ice in the river.
Yet not much work for my hands out-of-
doors. Roses were pruned and vines tied
up when the leaves fell; and now I can find
only a little mending here and there. We
have had furious winds lately, and some few
things have broken loose; and the covering

of my tulips and hyacinths is torn and ragged at the edges, with a clear hole in spots. They must have a new spread of leaves, without waiting for the snow blanket which may not come.

In-doors there is not much plant work either. A few bulbs are pushing up their shoots, and so are candidates for water and warmth; but while I was away, they were all left in a room which grew dangerously cold for anything *but* bulbs, and of course they made slow progress. I should except my double Roman P. narcissus, which ran up and up as if it were trying to reach the sun that way. It is coming into bloom now, just opening out; but ran itself too much out of breath to recover fairly.

Other plants crowd together on stands and tables or wherever they can get a place, waiting wearily for the spring. There are my seedling geraniums, a dozen or more,— with my especial variegated pet; and abutilon mesopotamicum, given by one friend, and a pretty little nameless green vine from

another. Then there is a small crowd of petunias and verbenas from last fall's cuttings,—fine kinds, that I did not wish to
lose. Then various plants struck in my sick
room last winter, from baskets of greenhouse
beauties brought by kind friends. French
lavender, and a tea rose, and two or three
specimens of Solanum jas. A wee Cape jes-
samine too, which as it hasn't died through
the summer, may perchance take heart
and grow—sometime. Then there is my
Chinese primrose. It was given to me with
the kind wish to help fill the place of some
frosted plants of mine; but has never done
itself much credit. When I had borne with
this state of things for a while, I set to work
to find out the reason; and if Mr. Henderson's directions for growing Chinese prim-
roses *could* be exactly reversed, surely in
this case they had been ! A glazed pot; solid clay soil that would retain every new
drop of water that ever came to it, without
letting go one of the old ; and large earth-
worms enough to make one think of an In-

dian juggler with his snakes. I'm not par-
tial to earth-worms. They are one little
drawback to the pleasure of gardening.

The plants in general looked very peaked
when I came home; first from being shut
up in a cold room, but much more from being
shut up in a hot one, where they were well
nigh killed with kindness. I bear freezing so
much better than roasting, myself, that I
gave them full sympathy. Water and light
and cool air, with a little fresh soil and clipping, have improved their appearance; and
as the room to which I first removed them
is still too warm and dry with its stove-heat,
I have devoted one window and a large
slice of our little study to flower stands, and
the rest retire into private life in a room
of no particular temperature; there to
" worry through " the winter, as somebody
(I think Mr. Henderson) calls it.

This being the time of year which the
cactus tribe choose for their long sleep, I
have left my two plants of that persuasion
on a tall cabinet in the warmest place I can

find; giving them no wáter at all, except just enough now and then to keep the earth from turning to absolute dust.

Except among the bulbs, you cannot expect many flowers at this season. At a temperature of less than sixty degrees, few house-plants will bloom; so florists say; and the rooms which come up to that in cold weather, are almost certain to be too close and dry for the plants. If buds form, they will probably drop off in a very disappointing way. Therefore keep your pets in good health, and yourselves in good patience. When we are able to build a little winter addition to our Fairyland, in the shape of a tiny greenhouse where we can syringe and shower and " make a muss " to our heart's content, *then* we may hope for roses at midwinter. For you see *then* we can afford to get the syringe too. And our greenhouse will not be a costly affair, with all the modern improvements; but a lovely little bow window opening out of our sitting room or breakfast room. Glass on all sides;

glazed doors also dividing it from the room ; and looking if possible full to the south or south-east. In cold weather with the glass doors open, and window shutters to help at night, and the sun to help by day, your greenhouse will keep warm with little trouble. And as the sun gains power, closed doors or an open window will do all the regulating. And your sitting room will be pretty as it never was before. Neither would the cost be so very much. Why a single " switch " (of the right colour) would do the work!

Meanwhile, pending all this, give your plants clean faces whenever your can. If there is a shower bath in the house, set it running—not quite full on—and pass your plants rapidly through the fall, one by one. If not, draw a cloth or paper tight round and over the top of the pot, to keep the earth in, and dip each plant head first in a basin of clean fresh water. You can hardly think how either process will revive them.

And now the catalogues begin to come in,—at a good time, when there is little other work to do. What are you going to plant? It is not very safe to make lists for other people, therefore get a good catalogue and choose for yourself. Study too, at the same time with names and colours, the nature of your soil and climate; for though as Education once said to Nature, "something may be done by taking pains enough," yet it is well to know *what* pains will be needful. But especially make yourself well acquainted with the catalogue, so as to leave no room for regrets.

Catalogues! Catalogues!—what bewildering things they are! How they do pile up epithets and suggestions and images; heaping "lovely blues," and "creamy whites," and "intense reds," and "clear yellows," and "rosy pinks," and "desirable contrasts," just to turn the heads of people who cannot get everything. There is a saying in the family that where other people read novels, *I* study catalogues—and it is a good deal so.

2*

But it's a matter requiring the most profound study!

Remember, in passing, that *some* of these catalogue colours will fade,—that cannot be helped. What certain florists call "blue," you put down as "purplish,"—what they call "black," is to your eyes only invisible red. Especially is this true of novelties, and the foreign descriptions of the same; which are generally got up *very* "regardless of expense."

What shall I get? How shall I have most show and sweetness with the least cost? For *what I can afford,* must come even before what I want. One novelty will buy from five to ten old favourites: yet the novelties are so enticing! Not the millionaire class—five dollars or so per seed—but those that are at least within sight of my purse. One or two of them I must have just for zest and flavour. But shall I try again some few that have thwarted me before? Shall I plant those that do not quite relish my soil and climate, or only the good little flowers that dress for themselves under all circumstances?

Plenty of these there must be, at all events. Phlox and verbenas and sweet peas and stocks and asters and pansies and balsams; with mignonette everywhere, and sweet alyssum in spots; and sweet scabious and sweet sultan for the scent of present fragrance and the perfume of old times. Poppies, too, for we were close friends once, when they were taller—or I was shorter!—peers in the old spring-time, frequenting the gravel walks together, and nearer of a height than we shall ever be again. And I find (curiously enough) that other people seem to have the same sort of recollections, only *they* have not been true to their early friendships. I have seen one and another stop by my poppy beds with a little cry of pleasure that came near being pain.

"Oh, poppies!" they say,—and hang over the little red faces with a sort of tender interest which poppies in themselves have not often the credit of inspiring. No—they

have gone out of fashion,—even the great
double many coloured and many-named poppies; and I doubt if one of the happy posses-
sors of glass and gardeners would have the
moral courage to admit a poppy upon his
grounds, much as he may enjoy meeting the
family at the house of a mutual friend.   But
our Fairyland has a place for everything we
want!

Therefore have as many pinks as you can
find room for; from the old, old, pink-faced,
sweet-breathed, double, fringed beauties,
that bed themselves in a mat of blue-green
foliage, and make up for blooming but once
a year, by being the fairest things there are
when they bloom.   From these, through
all the varieties you can, up to the stately
"Heddewigs" and "diadems."   By the way
it is simple folly to call a pink anything *but*
a pink.   They're no more like 'dianthus,'
than I am like a cricket.   To quote Mr.
Weller—'Wot's the use o' callin' a young
'ooman a 'wenus,' or a 'griffin?'"

Get some carnation seed too, that the

plants may be growing for next year. They will not bloom this. And petunias are sure to be useful, for they will thrive and be splendid in any season and in any place.

Then how beautiful last year was my Gaillardia Josephus! I must have it again. And the little blue asperula—a novelty of last year, as the catalogues say—was pretty enough, in spite of dry weather, to have another chance. Tropeolum King of the Tom Thumbs, and T. King Theodore, have also been very brilliant. I waited three years, I believe, for King Theodore to come down within reach of my purse, but have taken much comfort in him since.

Shall I give one more trial to Abronia?— little witch!—so highly recommended, so generally praised, but (for me) so intractable? We have been at issue for at least three seasons, and yet I don't like to be worsted! Shall I try conclusions once more with my favorite lupius, which (by way of being singular) seem not to like this Island of Shahweetah. Shall I be tempted

by a lily, " well preserved for spring planting," while yet I know that fall is *the* time?
How many tuberoses can I afford?—and
shall I indulge myself with a new gladiolus?

There—I have brought you into a laby-
rinth, and can do nothing but leave you to
find your way out alone.

FEBRUARY.

Brilliant hopes, all woven in gorgeous tissues,
Flaunting gaily in the golden light;
Large desires, with most uncertain issues,
Tender wishes, blossoming at night.

—Longfellow.

HAVE your seeds come? Mine have.
Such a delightful package of little
packages!—each full of mystery, each rust-
ling gently with promise. And O, what
mystery it is!

Look into your little paper of "mixed
petunia" seed,—holding your breath the
while; for the grains are so fine that you
could breathe them all away, so small and
light that they are hard to manage, with
the best of care. There they lie in a small
dark heap, each seed just like its fellow
seed to look at, yet with a whole different
existence in each. In one is wrapped the
glory of a full crimson flower, three inches

across; in another lies perdu a blossom of pink, with a broad green border; hid away in the next brown grain of dust is a white blossom, all striped and flamed with purple; while the next will open out upon the world in rose-colour, with a pure white throat. One will be plain-edged, and one will be fringed; one will be plain-coloured, and the next full of spots and veins, and the next as double as a rose; and the one little grain that stays fast in the corner of the bag, holds, perhaps, some new variety, now lost to the gardening world!

Take a peep in among my pansy seed. Can you guess which little brown flat speck will give you "sky-blue," or "violet," or the "king of the blacks"? Can you tell among the phlox seed *Leopoldii* from *Radowitzii*, or a "brilliant scarlet" from a "deep blood purple"? Which canna seed will give you a "brilliant red" spike of flowers, and which a "superb yellow?" Which of these portulaca seeds, looking now like mites of quicksilver, will open out into "gold colour?" which into "crimson?" which into "white-striped?" Each little grain of this dust which we call seed, has in itself both root and leaf and profusion of bloom; and the particular mite which I have just brushed off from the tip of my finger, may be the finest "possibility" in all the lot!

MAPLE SEED CUT TO SHEW THE FOLDED PLANT.   PLANT TAKEN OUT.

O never ending wonder and mystery of Gen. 1: 10, 12!—"Whose seed is in itself, after its kind." O standing "miracle of flowers and trees!"—so perfect as to be "very good" in the eyes of the Lord himself,"—it will never cease to be marvellous in our eyes.

Now what will you do with these little packets of wonders? To begin with, go over your list, catalogue in hand, to note carefully which kinds of seed must be sown

3

in the house, and which must be left for the open border; as well as those that *may* be

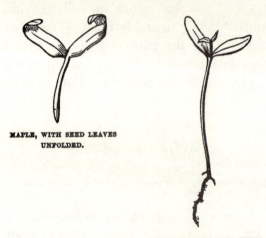

MAPLE, WITH SEED LEAVES
UNFOLDED.

MAPLE, SHEWING THE FIRST
PAIR OF LEAVES.

planted there, if it is more convenient. For some flowers need transplanting, and some will not like it; and some, if they are not sown early, will take a year to bloom. Separate your seeds first according to this rule. Then from the house-set, take out the hardiest, and let them have attention first; because *very* tender things must be set out

so late, that they need not be sown very
early. Except canna, and datura, and a
few others of which the catalogue will tell
you, that are shy of blooming the first
year, and so must be got in as early as possible.

First of all, then, put your canna seeds in
scalding water, and leave them in a hot
place (not boiling) for twelve hours or so,
while you attend to other matters.

What soil have you got for planting? If
you made no preparation last fall, you cannot
have "rotted sods," nor some other excellent things that need time and care to make
them good; yet if you live in the country,
the want can be easily made up. In town,
the shortest way is to buy sixpence worth
of prepared soil at the nearest greenhouse.
In the country, take basket and trowel and
go off to the woods—deciduous woods, not
evergreen, if you have the choice—and
there pry into the little hollows, among
rocks and tree-roots. Scrape off last year's
leaves which lie on top, and the leaves of

the year before, and the year before that, which come next; and when you have thus disposed of several withered generations, you will come to a little black, fresh, perfectly-decayed mould. Not much in a place, perhaps, but the places are many; and there is nothing, with me, that has proved so good for the growth of seeds, as this same leaf mould from the woods. You may use it alone, or with a mingling of common earth, or a little sand.

Having got the soil, the next thing is what to put it in. What is to hold your little seed beds in the house? All the florists, without exception, I believe, say: "Never use pots." And I only answer such high authority with the old words: "When you can't do as you would, you must do as you can." Little seed boxes, sawed in two at a four-inch depth, are capital; and soap boxes with the like treatment, are first-rate. But it is not every lover of flowers that has strength and time to cut up old boxes or make the new. It is not every masculine

head of a family that will give *his* strength
and time to "trumpery." And seeds will
grow, and grow well, in flower-pots, if only
they have the right sort of care. Earthen
seed-pans (a kind of broad, shallow flower-
pot) are, I think, on the whole, about the
best thing I ever used,—light and manage-
able, and large enough not to let the earth
dry too fast. And there is a great system
of indemnity in this world. Soap boxes are
good, no doubt, Mr. Henderson ; but if they
have to be carried about from window to
window and room to room, to catch the
sun or follow the fire, then, you see, there
is a qualification to their excellence.

Well, take the best you can get,—then
prepare your mould by sifting. And as
you and I have not always a nest of riddles
at hand, let me tell you that a twenty-five
cent wire ladle will do extremely well for
the first rough sifting ; while a small wire
sieve, for the like extravagant price, will finish up the work in a quite superior manner.
Even a cinder sifter can be made to help.

3*

Fill your boxes or pots about half full of the rough sifting that remain in the sieve, and then fill to within an inch of the top with the finest of the mould ; shake the pots lightly, smooth down the mould with a light pressure, and sow your seeds.

Now in all gardening matters one. must use plenty of common sense. You will see at a glance, if you think as well as look, that all seeds must not be planted alike. Some are large, like canna and balsams and thunbugia, and need to be down in the ground a half inch or more. Then others, smaller or lighter, like verbenas, must have less covering ; and when you get to the little dust-seeds—petunias and poppies and portulacca—make the surface of the earth very smooth, scatter the seeds over, and press them gently down. That is covering enough. The soil should be damp, but not wet, when you sow seeds ; and after sowing it is good to give the whole a gentle sprinkling, and then to cover the pots with an old pane of glass if you have one at

leisure. If not, a folded newspaper will do
very well, and keep the seeds from drying
too fast, before they have a chance to start.
Much watering for the first few days is apt
to wash the smaller seeds out of place and
out of sight. Take notice, too, in your
planting, that all thin, flat seeds,—such as
stocks, for instance,—need less covering of
earth than those which are round and hard.
Keep your pots and boxes in a warm room,
but not too hot, where the seeds will have
gentle forcing; only the cannas may be set
in the warmest place you can find. On the
water kettle of a stove is very good.

If there is verbena seed among your packages, that *must* have fresh soil. Whatever
the others can put up with, give the verbenas what they want. Not earth taken
from a garden, in which whole races of
plants have lived and died for years; but
earth from the woods, or the crumbly
mould of decayed sods, or scrapings from
the rich spots and corners of a pasture-land.
The under surface of each new sod you can

take up, has a *very* little that is very good. Such new "stuff," as the gardeners call it, is best for all seeds, but indispensable for verbenas. Dexter Snow, of Chicopee—great authority on verbenas—says there is no use in trying to grow them in old soil; and my experience certainly bears him out. The seeds will not start well; the plants will not be strong; and the bed of bloom which you *ought* to have from each verbena will resolve itself into a poor, scraggy, straggling plant, a burden to itself and to everybody that sees it.

Have fresh soil for your verbenas. And even when you set them out in the garden— unless you can dig up new beds for them every year—take out a few spadefuls of earth from the old bed where a plant is to go, and fill in with new, rich stuff from the woods or the pasture.

Most people, I think, choose rather to buy the plants than the seed; and to be absolutely *sure* of fine varieties, and special varieties, that is of course the best way. So, also, if you want whole beds of white or purple or crimson. And it is quite true that young verbenas are much given to "miffs" and freaks, and do not always consider existence worth striving for. But they are very interesting seedlings to me, because they "sport" so freely; and I never know just what I shall have, and enjoy all the pleasure of expectation and novelty and surprise. I said they were of uncertain disposition, but that is only while they are in the seed-leaf. Once started in the world with a pair of rough leaves, and verbenas will defy most things. Before that, you must watch them a little. Sometimes the young plant comes up with the old seed for a head-piece,—not carried loosely, bean-fashion, but worn with a very tight fit; and then (perhaps because the air of the room is too dry) the seed maintains its hold, and keeps the leaves in prison. If this lasts dangerously long (don't wait till the little plant begins to hang its heavy head), take small sharp scissors and clip off the tip end of the seed, steadying the plant all the while with a spare finger. Generally then, with a break once made, the leaves muster strength and finish the work, and the plant is not a bit the worse. The seed-leaves will be a little nipped at the ends, but the true leaves will be quite unhurt; unless indeed you have clipped too close.

People who sow a dozen packets of seed will smile at my directions: people who sow but one will understand.

Keep your seed-pans moist, but not wet. "Sprinkle every day," Mr. Henderson says,—but sprinkle cautiously. Do you know how? It is an easy matter if you have all appliances,— a "sprinkler," or "syringe," with all the modern improvements. But a brass syringe is costly, and I never saw a tin one yet that was worth house room. You must educate your fingers. For no "mist" will go up out of the ground for your flowers as it did for Eve's,—you must imitate *her* Fairyland as best you may. I have watered a great many little seed-beds from the ends of my

fingers, letting the drops glide softly off,
and holding my fingers quite close to the
soil ; for if the drops fall from too great a
height they pack and harden it. If the
seeds are large, and not easily disturbed,
hold your left hand close over the pot, hollow it slightly, and pour the water slowly in
there ; letting it trickle softly down between
the closed fingers. Another expedient (of
a professed gardener, this time) is to take
a clean paint brush, dip it in water, and
draw it through your hand in such a fashion
that the drops fall in a shower of fine spray.
But this needs practice.

In the intervals of seed business, look
over your potted plants ; for they will begin
to wake up now, thinking of new leaves, and
possible blossoms : therefore give them all
the encouragement you can. Nip off the
leaves that are faded, prune in unruly
shoots, see if any need re-potting. For
when the old pot is getting crowded with
roots, it is then best to move. But let
the change be always to a pot just one size

larger. When there is no need of repotting, turn off some of the top soil, and fill up with new; and this needs no fine sifting. The plants may have more water too, as the spring draws on; and all the sunshine that can be had.

How softly the season advances now!—how exquisite is the unbending of nature!—Even with ice and snow still in sight, there is a change in the whole look of the world. The light is different, and more tender; the clouds roll up in softer lines; and even in the wind—cold as it is yet—there comes the strange wild scent of swelling buds. And the phœbes chant softly to each other; and the sun sends warm persuasive glances to which even the soberest heart must yield.

Every day I set my plants out in our little glazed piazza for a taste of early summer; and stand there myself, to watch them. How they love the sun!—seeming to yearn towards it; even as I, last winter, in my sunless sick room, used to lay my face close against the window frame, to catch—slantwise—one little ray of the blessed sunshine.

Even so my plants lean towards the light, stretching forth their hands to grasp it and bring it home.

Do you see?—it is their life, their joy, their rest. The pale leaves take strength and colour, the drooping buds lift up their heads; the new shoots spring forth to grow.

"I don't know"—said a poor Scotch girl, when the Session before whom she was examined doubted whether she "knew enough" to join the church; "I can't tell about that. May be I don't know enough. But as a flower turns to the sun, so my heart turns to the Lord Jesus."

4

MARCH.

Daffy-down-dilly came up in the cold,
    Through the brown mould,
Although the March breezes blew keeu on her face,
Although the white snow lay in many a place.

Daffy-down-dilly had heard under ground
    The sweet rushing sound
Of the streams, as they burst off their white winter chains,—
Of the whistling Spring winds and the pattering rains.

"Now then," thought Daffy, deep down in her heart, ——
    "It's time I should start !"
So she pushed her soft leaves through the hard frozen
    ground,
Quite up to the surface, and there she looked round.

There was snow all about her,—grey clouds overhead,—
    The trees all looked dead.
Then how do you think Daffy-down-dilly felt,
When the sun would not shine and the ice would not melt?

"Cold weather !" thought Daffy, still working away :
    "The earth's hard to-day !
There's but a half inch of my leaves to be seen,
And two-thirds of that is more yellow than green !"

" I can't do much yet—but I'll do what I can.
    It's well I began !
For unless I can manage to lift up my head,
The people will think that the Spring herself's dead."

So, little by little, she brought her leaves out,
    All clustered about ;
And then her bright flowers began to unfold,
Till Daffy stood robed in her Spring green and gold.

O Daffy-down-dilly ! so brave and so true !
    I wish all were like you !
So ready for duty in all sorts of weather,
And holding forth courage and beauty together.

I LIKE to begin early, even with the out-
of-door work. Using caution of course,
and judgment; but still following close on
the retiring footsteps of the snow, and dis-
puting the ground inch by inch with the
frost. Pleasure is gained, if nothing else.

Of course regular digging while the earth
is wet and cold, will be of little use,—if you
dig it now, it will just dry in lumps and
clods that will give you endless trouble. It
is very heavy work, besides. But you can
rake and dress and "fuss," to your heart's
content,—transplanting and arranging and

considering ; and if the digging waits a little, the hardy perennials will have their
heads above ground, and so miss the chance
of being decapitated by your spade; and
many self-sown annuals will spring up,
ready to your hand for transplanting. And
besides, — a matter of much importance
where you do your own digging,—the la-
bour will be not half, if the ground is dry
and crumbly and *friable* : if it *works* well, as
experts say.

Do you do your own digging ?—and do
you know how ? It is such pretty work !—
and by no means so tiresome as hoeing.

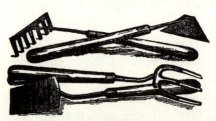

SET OF LADIES' GARDEN TOOLS.

A light spade is the first essential,—sharp
and bright and clean from all soil of the last

digging. Then ground in good condition : then, patience to do very little at a time, till you get used to the work. If you fail to use this last little tool, the chance is that you will lay yourself up with a lame back and an extreme disgust for digging. But it will be your fault, not the spade's. You can lame yourself just as thoroughly with a too-long first ride on horseback, or pull in the boat.

Having then all essentials, begin joyous-ly !—with the scent of the fresh grass and the fresh earth circling all round you, and blue birds charming your eyes, and song sparrows cheering you on. And if you *can* persuade one of those useful articles called men to go round each flower bed with a stronger foot and spade, trimming the grass edging where it has encroached, before you begin, your work will be all the easier.

The first rule seems very simple. Begin at one end. Or if the bed is round and end-less, begin at one side. And when you have begun, go steadily on, *in that line.* Did you

4*

ever see a woman begin to scrub in the middle of the floor, or at the door of exit? Very well: *don't* do that: you must not walk over the ground you have dug.

Begin at one end,—and open a narrow furrow quite across the bed, taking out the earth and conveying it quite to the other end. If the bed is but small, a strong, skilled hand can easily throw the earth there at once, spadeful by spadeful; but it needs strength; and so Mrs. Loudon says, that a light wheelbarrow is the best means of transport. And I should say that too; but I tried so long in vain to get a light wheelbarrow myself, that I am afraid to call it an essential. A basket will do instead.

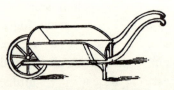

LADIES' WHEELBARROW.

The furrow once opened, dig across the line of earth that comes next to it, taking moderate spadefuls, but going down as deep as you can; and turn each spadeful of earth quite upside down into the empty furrow. Go regularly on in this way, till the whole bed is finished, being careful to break and mix the earth well as you go, and also to pick out any large stones. Common weeds and rubbish may be buried at the bottom of your furrows; but pull out all the sorrel, root and branch. *That* will grow, sideways and endways and all ways; and from almost a foot deep.

If the bed is small, you need not begin to rake till it is all dug; but in a large bed, the best way is to rake from time to time, as soon as you have ready a strip of two or three feet wide. Hold the handle of the rake high, and use it lightly; breaking lumps and bringing all the surface to a fine crumbly state. Let the centre of the bed be a little higher than the sides (more or less, according to your soil) and be careful to leave no small hills and valleys as you go. If the ground needs manure, that must

be spread evenly over the bed before you
begin the digging ; and no manure should be
used, of any kind, that is not well decayed
and in a dry, crumbly state that will let it
mix easily with the mould.

If you want to draw earth from one part
of the bed to another with your rake, *then*
hold the handle low.

To go back to our verbenas. As soon as
you see the plants fairly up, give them plenty of light and sunshine ; else they will run
up slim and tall like a boy that has out-
grown his strength ; and be what the gardeners call " drawn." And as soon as the
first little rough leaves begin to appear, pot
the seedlings off singly in very small pots—
the smaller the better. All house seedlings
should be treated in the same way, if you
have small pots enough. If not, then use a
larger size, and put three plants in each ;
setting them round the edge at even distances apart. Then when they are to be set
in the open ground, turn out the whole ball
of earth into your hand, and neatly break

it into three, having a plant in each. If
you are careful, the roots will be almost as
little disturbed as if each seedling had its
own pot. And by the way, in choosing
small pots for this work, get those that
are narrow and deep rather than broad,
— roots need most room in that direction.

Suppose only one plant in the seed pan is
ready for transplanting,—some small geranium or verbena that has pushed on ahead
of its fellows. Then take a very small kitch-
en teaspoon, or a narrow flat bit of stick, a
little sharpened at one end, and carefully
dig up the plant that is ready. If you put
your stick well down to the bottom of the
seed pan, you can take up a seedling with
all the earth that fairly belongs to it, and
make no disturbance that can matter to the
other plants. Have a small clean pot at
hand, with a potsherd over the hole and a
little earth on that; set stick and plant gently down in the middle; and without remov-
ing the stick put in earth enough to hold up

the plant. Draw out your stick gently, fill up the pot to within a half inch of the top, strike it lightly on the table to "firm" the earth, water slowly and moderately; and then if the earth has sunk away too much, add more. Keep your seedling for a few days "warm and close," the florists say, until it is "established;" then give it plenty of sunshine, and air by degrees, turning your plant often, lest it should not be "of a round mind." And do not forget to fill up the hole in the seed-pan bed, with a spoonful of fresh earth.

In all my talk about plants in pots, I believe I have said nothing of the insects which sometimes trouble them,—partly, indeed, because I almost forgot their existence. In our cool, fresh rooms, with open fires and plenty of air, the plants enjoy themselves much better than the insects; and I rarely see one. But in close, stove-heated houses, the advantage is all the other way.

Almost everybody who has had a few roses

or geraniums to care for, has made acquaintance at some time or other with the delicate, pretty, mischievous little green fly, or
aphis. Probably most have seen (on their
own plants or other people's) a tender rose
shoot, a sweet geranium leaf, so covered
with these little interlopers as to be simply
disgusting. And though hand-picking may
have made a clearance for the time, yet the
ranks were always filled and refilled, in ex-
haustless measure. Quietly sapping the juices
of your plants, and spoiling the look of all
that they did not eat, so you have seen
them. Well, for your comfort and encouragement, Mr. Henderson says that this
small mischief-maker should never be seen.
Of course it follows that he *need* not. The
best greenhouse preventive seems to be
thorough fumigation;—one speck of sense
the aphis has in its small head—it does not
like tobacco. Smoke your little greenhouse
two or three times a week; and when you
can stand the smell long enough yourself to
go and look, you will find that the aphis

tribe have disappeared—or not appeared—
as the case may be.

A sweeter, easier remedy for those who
live in their greenhouse, is pure cold water.
A vigorous shower bath, at short intervals,
is the best thing I ever tried.

Worse than the green aphis, but not so
well-known, is the red spider. A minute
speck of scarlet,—too small to be noticed,
but working infinite harm. You can trace
them by their work; for after *their* feeding,
the plant leaves turn brown as if they had
been slightly scorched. I lost almost a
whole set of fine seedling calceolarias once
in that way, before I ever guessed what was
the matter. Water is the great remedy
here,—showering, syringing, washing the
leaves; whatever you can do best; and remember that the hotter and dryer the air
where you keep your plants, the more
danger they are in from red spider.

The verbena mite, or "rust"—another
creature known chiefly by its work, is beyond the reach of most remedies, bedding

itself in the very substance of the leaf. The best preventive is to keep your plants in vigorous growth.

"I had a lot of about 500 heliotropes," says Mr. Henderson, "growing in two-inch pots; one half of which were, in September, shifted into three-inch pots. They were kept side by side, and treated in all respects the same. Those shifted, of course, with increased food, grew vigorously and strong, while the unshifted remained comparatively stunted; and to-day, Dec. 1st, the 'black rust' shows itself on nearly every plant, and the microscope shows on every affected leaf hundreds of these insects, feeding like sheep on a pasture field, while on the shifted plants none whatever can be found."*

Keep growing,—is safe counsel for your plants as well as yourself.

Mealy bug needs no description. You may never see him,—if you do, pick him off. If he *will* stay, give him a dose of whale-oil

* Practical Floriculture.

soapsuds. Though this is not very safe for very tender plants.

If there is an oleander in your collection, you may find the scale insect on some of the stems. It is ugly, but not very harmful,— hand-picking and washing the stems with soapsuds are the best cure.

Meantime, with all this house care, do not forget your sweet peas out-of-doors. Plant them as soon as the ground will work. Frost in the air won't hurt them. It is a good way to set whatever support they are to have, *before* planting. Make sure that the stick or trellis is in firm and upright; then plant your peas, pretty thick, and not a bit less than four inches deep. Never fear, they'll come up; and their roots will be beyond the reach of summer heats.

Some other things should be sown as early as possible in the open ground,—candy-tuft, larkspur, poppies, mignonnette, lupins, sweet alyssum, clarkia, and such hardy annuals. Directions say, put them at once where they are to remain, as most of these

dislike transplanting; and they do certainly
need extra care. But I think I have transplanted every one of those named above, and
had them do well. One of the first things I
do in the spring, when the ground is cleared and softened, is to examine my flower
beds very closely, to find out any stray
seedlings that may have come up, and to
move them to prepared quarters. Of
course this examination must be *before* the
ground is stirred.

Dig the place for these, or for seeds, *not*
when it is wet; making it fine and soft;
stake out a charmed circle a foot or so broad
with neat slender sticks; and there sow
your seeds—not too deep. Be careful to
cover them according to the size of the
seeds—sweet peas are the only exception ;
and let the covering be too shallow rather
than too deep. Seeds covered too lightly
may come up (so says Mrs. Loudon) by dint
of very favourable weather; but seeds covered too deep never can. Press down the
earth gently the first thing, and the last

thing; and stick a label in the middle or at one side of the patch. Else you may get two sets of poppies "cheek by jowl," and red, white, and blue, in anything but harmonious confusion. Some gardeners say it is well to cover the seed patch for a few days with a bit of board or an empty flower pot. It may be,—I have never tried it. But remember neither to dig nor sow nor transplant just after a heavy rain. The earth will dry in clods, and give you great trouble.

Some time this month you must uncover your bulbs. The middle of March is generally my time; but that must vary a little with season and place. Let no careless hand touch the beds; for the shoots are many of them well up by this time, and the brush and leaves must be taken off very gently. Then dress the surface of the earth with light trowel work, so as to loosen and smooth and put the whole in neat order; being very careful not to injure the shoots that are not yet up. Give relief to the tulips

that have come up with a dry leaf round
their necks, and tighten any labels that the
frost has thrown out. You need not be
uneasy because the shoots look yellow instead of green; they will take their right
colour when they have had a little sunshine
and fresh air. And the night frosts will not
hurt them, nor even a spring snow. Dress
the ground and leave them alone, until
their heads of bloom need tying up.

APRIL.

Do you know what Spring is doing?
Little children, do you know
She has carried off the icicles,
And swept away the snow?
The soft air comes to fan her,
And the birch hangs out his banner,
And the squirrel-cup peeps boldly from his brown leaf
    bed below.

IF there is a month in the year when
everything wants doing at once, and
nothing is willing to wait, I suppose it is
this same rainbow month of April. Every
individual seed and plant is in a hurry, and
you must have a good deal of self-control to
escape the breathless contagion; for with
your pets on the jump, how shall you give
them slow and quiet attention? Yet they
need it,—need shading and repressing sometimes; for it will not do for them to get
ahead of the season. The storm-nursed lit-

tle candytufts and alyssums that have come
up out-of-doors on their own responsibility,
will fight the frost and live it through; but
your thin-skinned house seedlings are quite
another matter. *Their* tissues are delicate
with warmth and petting; and unless they
are hardened off *before* they are set out, the
hardening process will prove fatal. You remember the little girl who went to school
with the tears freezing on her cheeks and
her mittens in her pocket. Being asked the
cause of this arrangement, she replied that
she "wanted to be tough." Well—you
must "toughen" your plants more gently
than that. When they are well up, set the
seed-box further from the stove; and when
the potted seedlings are well established,
give them cooler air, and more of it, from
day to day, that they may be ready to brave
the outer world.

Do you know, unscientific people who
love flowers, how it is that your pets freeze
to death? It was a delightful discovery to
me, when I first understood it. Each plant,

and each part of a plant, you must remember, is made up of minute little cells, separated by only a wall of thin tissue. As the plant grows, the cells expand to their full size, and then divide themselves in two by throwing across from side to side a new little wall of tissue. In its turn each half of the divided cell stretches out to full proportions and divides again ; and so the process goes on. Now these cells are not emp-

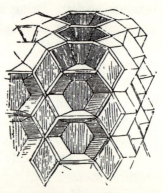

SECTION OF MAPLE ROOT TO SHOW THE CELLS.

ty, but are full of a thin sort of mucilage, with often a little nucleus of matter still more solid. If then, the cold is intense enough to freeze this mucilage, it swells out, of course, as you know liquids do in freezing, and bursts through the thin walls of the cell. And if this once happens, the plant—or that part of it—is dead beyond recovery. But hardy plants have stronger tissues, and the frost does them no harm ; except perhaps to a new shoot here and there which we call "imperfectly ripened,"—not having yet attained the full thickness of its tissues. Do you see now, how if your seedlings are sent straight from the stove to the garden, their tissues are too tender to stand anything ? Whereas, by careful hardening, the walls of the cells will have grown thick and strong, and the plants may be set out with little danger.

A grave question comes up in many minds at this time of year, as to the best arrangement of flower beds,—a nice question, too ; having much to do with the results so gleefully expected from our little packets of seed. Yet I do not want to give much real advice on the subject. It is well enough to study

plans and designs, if you like ; but then de-
cide quite independently, and do not be
driven or lured from your own choice and
taste by any such words as " old-fashioned "
or "indispensable ;" else you may find yourself, like poor Rosamond, digging a pond
which will be " quite full and very useful "
in rainy weather only. Use your judgment
and common sense,—they are Taste's two
best under-gardeners. The arrangement
which is very fine for one piece of ground,
suiting its size and characteristics, may be
quite lost in another; and figures which
make a beautiful mosaic in skilful hands,
are often mere disorder and confusion,
where want of practice or want of time
leaves them to their own devices, untrim-
med and uncared for. Therefore, study
your time first of all, and choose no plan
which will require more of that than you
can give.

If you are unlimited in this respect; if
you have an eye for colour as well as form ;
if neither your pains nor your patience are

likely to give out; then you may have a
very splendid show with a geometric flower
garden,—where all the beds are laid out in
exact shapes, and with a certain reference to
each other; the whole forming a pattern of
coloured embroidery upon the green turf.
In this case each bed must be filled with a
single colour and a single kind of flower,
the compact, close-growing sorts being
chosen, and those which are of constant and
abundant bloom. A mere border line of a
different colour is admissible round each
bed; but it will not make the figure so full
and perfect as where simple masses of colour are used. For full effect, such a garden
should be on ground a little lower than the
house, so that the whole may be seen together. One of the finest situations I ever
saw, was where the house stood on an up-
springing rise of ground; and quite at the
foot, a little to one side but all in sight, lay
the garden.

Geometric beds need to be very carefully
planned and marked out, before a thing is

planted; and they always show best with grass between,—"laid down in turf," as the books say: though of course box or other edgings may be used, and the walks made of gravel. But whatever divides the beds must be kept in the most precise order. So must the flowers themselves. Plant or sow them rather thicker than needful, at first, and then thin out from time to time, so as to have strong, hardy plants, that will cover the whole ground. Then, as they grow, keep them rigourously within bounds; clip and train and fasten back, and let nothing stray over the limits by even so much as a bud. A geometric flower garden must have military line-and-rule precision; neither visiting nor "followers" can be allowed; and the pretty wandering blossoms that go roaming about with such fair effect in other places, have no business here. Neither must you let plants have entirely their own up-and-down way,—prune the aspiring shoots of geraniums, and keep everything close and bushy and *at home*. Keep watch also of your edgings, lest they encroach in irregular fashion here and there, and so spoil your pattern. Choose and sort your colours carefully, giving heed to the contrasts. Mrs. Loudon advises that the design be first drawn and coloured on paper, where alterations are easy. And then throughout the season see that your beds have not only care and clipping, but also water—from your hands, if the clouds fail; lest brown plants and empty beds take the place of bright patches of colour. This it is, more than anything else perhaps, which makes geometric flower gardens such a success in England and (so often) such a failure here: the English climate is so much more favourable.

To say truth, I never saw any "bedding" system in *our* climate amount to much more than beds of tinted green; and I never even guessed how superb it might be, till an English lady showed me a water-colour sketch of a certain English country house. Quiet and brown itself, the house had for a fore-

ground a lawn of living velvet, and, upon
that, flower-beds that were like spots of
flame or bits of sky,—mere miracles of colour.

"And then the turf"—remarked our
hostess,—"it is not all climate; but the turf
has been mowed and rolled and watered,
and mowed and rolled and watered, for a
hundred years!"

Another plan in great favour now, is to
ribband everything,—the flowers being set
in even lines along or around the bed, sort
beyond sort, and colour beyond colour.
The beds may be of any size or shape; but
the plants should vary in height, rising slowly from the outer edge to the centre or the
back. Let the trailers be at the very front,—
the little four-inch or six-inch beauties; then
the eight and twelve-inch; and so on back to
two, three, and four feet—or eight feet—if
you choose. Be careful of your colours here
also, and plant only free and constant bloomers; for you cannot easily get in among the
lines to replace one sort with another.

If you have plenty of room on your lawn,

if your lawn is kept always close-shaven, then small beds here and there upon it, filled with one single colour each, are very fair to see. But do not be persuaded to waste your roses in beds. I never saw a rose-bed yet that had half the beauty of a single fine specimen "left blooming alone," either in among other and lower flowers, or in a little dug-out patch by itself.

To mark out these simple beds you need only a long cord with a pointed stick tied to each end. Set one stick firm in the ground, where the centre of the bed should be, and with the other trace your circle. Then stake it well and evenly, ready for cutting in the turf, or edging in the open ground. To make an exact oval, set both sticks in line, a little nearer together than the proposed length of the bed; wind up the cord until it is *just* that length; and then with a third stick draw out the cord as far as it will reach on all sides, marking as you go, till you come round to the point where you began.

And now what shall I say about the old-fashioned garden?—much talked against, much laughed at, by most people who have "facilities." Yet for those who have not, it after all often the best; needing less time, less skill, less knowledge of form and colour; and giving results that are sweet at least, if they are not wonderful. Few directions are called for here. Fair, rich confusion is all the aim of an old-fashioned flower garden, and the greater the confusion, the richer. You want to come upon mignonnette in unexpected places, and to find sprays of heliotrope in close consultation with your roses, and geraniums sporting their uniforms like gay recruits off duty. Sweet peas bow to phloxes here, and the gladiolus straightens itself with harmless pride among its more pliant companions, and the little white sweet alyssum goes visiting all the day. There is the most exquisite propriety and good fellowship, with an utter absence of "deportment;" and the perennials that pass out of flower are kindly hid and merged by their

blooming neighbors, till their time of glory
comes round again. And if a sedate member of the Balm family shows its red head in
a corner, or a tall bush cranberry peeps over
the fence to display its strings of coral : even
if an old Corchorus surveys the beauties of
to-day, and gravely discourses of

" The times that used to was,"—

nobody is shocked, and the old bush is not
disturbed. No stiffness, no ceremony,—flowers, and not a garden,—this is the beauty of
the old style; yet even here taste and judgment will find work.

For instance, you will not shadow your
lively little verbenas with the stately growth
of a tall ricinus ; nor force the tea roses to
keep house near the marigolds. You will
not suffer a weed anywhere. Give the
small things a chance to be seen, and let
distance heighten the enchantment of those
that are tall and tree-like. Scatter your
colours broadcast indeed, and yet with a
certain thought and method ; have plenty
6*

of tufts of pure green, such as rose geraniums and the flowering grasses, with here and there a red achyranthes or mottled coleus to catch and hold the sun: and let fragrance abound everywhere. For this is much of the charm of the old garden,—not trim shapes, and inlaid figures, and gorgeous masses of colour; but rich, soft, mingled bloom, and tender tints, and wafts of nameless sweetness to every passer-by.

However your beds are laid out, however your flowers are distributed, remember to use great care in preparing the soil and putting in the seed. Then, when the seeds are in, use patience. For some will be slow to come up, taking a long while to awaken out of their brown sleep; and some will come up in a thin scattering fashion; because certain flowers ripen their seed unequally, and always give a large percentage of husks. Perhaps a few kinds will not come up at all. You may have covered them too deep; or a cold storm may have caught the little seedlings in the first moments of their growth, and chilled them past recovery ; or some unseen host of insect marauders may have quartered on them for a night, choosing your flower bed before all the world. Such things must happen now and then, and the best regulated families suffer.

It is good to reserve a little seed of various kinds—especially the smaller and more delicate—for a second planting in such emergencies: sometimes, too, one can fill the vacant places with the thinnings of another patch. Yet do not be in a hurry to conclude that the first planting has failed ; because, as I said, some seeds must have time ; and those wiry little things that hurry up as if they had slept all winter with one eye open, may mislead you concerning the rest. But however things go, take Mr. Vick's advice, and count the seeds that grow rather than those that fail,—letting no lament for what you have not, spoil the sweetness of what you have.

We had an old gardener once who had a

dexterous way of running his finger down into the flower pot or seed patch to see if the seeds were " coming;" but it is a bad plan for people of less experience. Let the seeds wait their time,—wait too, it may be, for clear sunshine or a shower of rain,—and then before you know it they will be up; some sooner, some later, each after its kind.

I tried a new way with my canna seeds this year, to find out whether they were coming up. They had steamed away on the top of the stove-kettle so long, that I began to have doubts on the subject, and resolved one day to try a change of stimulus and give them a little sunshine. So I took up the pot, carried it safely across one room, and dropped it full in the middle of the next! then looked about me in some dismay. For an electric shock wants at least to be applied judiciously, and with some regard to the strength of the patient. There lay the shattered pot, there was the warm black earth scattered far and wide; and there, sprinkled upon it, so to say, were three

brown canna seeds, each showing an unmis-
takable white root and the tip of a young
green leaf. Well, there was no use in driving them into seclusion again. I brought
little pots, and gave each seedling one; hiding the green shoot lightly beneath the soil,
that it might after all take its own time for
appearing. Then I searched out the rest
of the seeds, crumbling every black lump
of earth, sifting and examining with my fingers, finding the other three one by one.
But they were all in their original state of
blackness and hardness; and though I re-
planted them, giving them both steam and
sun, not one was kind enough to grow. The
first three flourished and made fine plants.

N. B.—In trying this experiment, it is
well to count your seeds before planting,
that you may know when you have picked
them all up.

MAY.

"O," said the little blades of grass,
    Growing up;
"O, how the spring hours pass,
    Butter-cup!
Winds come and whistle,
  And birds come and sing,
And the early time of life
  Is a very sunny thing!"

"Yes," said the buttercup, and bowed
    Very low;
"And joy cometh also from a cloud,
    As you know:
Soft April showers,
  And sweet drops of rain,
How they make our faces shine
When the sun comes out again!"

THE days pass, and the weeks gather them up, and still there is little change in our garden. Cold winds by day, and light frosts by night, rather chill the energies of young seedlings, and they are slow to venture forth into such an unpromising world.

But though we must confess, with the wonderful writer of the Biglow papers, that

> "Half our May's so awfully like mayn't,"—

yet who is not ready to follow him further, in his rejoicing over our seasons just
as they are?

> "Though I own up, I like our back'ard springs,
>   That kind o' haggle with their greens an' things,
>   An' when you most give up, 'ithout more words
>   Toss the fields full o' blossoms, leaves and birds."

It is dangerous to begin quoting from
such a book of beauties! I am tempted on.
But as Mr. Biglow himself remarks:

> "'Nuff sed."

Slow as the season is in its developing
process, invisible as is the growth which
your little plants do really make from day
to day, it is well that there is so much other work to do in the garden besides watching them. Work which cannot wait, and so
makes our waiting easier. First go over
the grass of lawn and edgings, and have
bare spots resodded or broken up and

sprinkled with grass seed and clover: even a light dressing of fine barn-yard manure will do much. All rubbish of sticks and stones—the drift of winter storms—should have been raked off long ago. Dig up any wild onions that show their presumptuous heads, getting the start of the grass; and if sorrel appears here and there, give it such a dusting with wood-ashes that it will be glad to hide. Just now, while merely in leaf, you notice it less; but by and by, when it is in flower, the red patches will spoil the lawn effect, pretty as they may be in themselves.

Put fresh gravel upon the walks wherever it is washed or worn away; and the Quaker storm, when it comes, will beat all down into smooth compactness.

In and about the flower beds, too, there is work. Honeysuckles need support and clipping, and roses need tying up. A tall-growing rose is twice as handsome if it is fast bound to a tall stake; then the buds start out on every side, and you have a pyramid of roses Prune off all the dead or half-dead

shoots, and all that have strayed into un-
gainly length ; cutting them back to a sound,
fresh bud. Above all, give them a thorough
application of whale-oil soap, to kill or keep
off the slugs ; unless indeed you have no
such pests on your roses ; and even then it
is safe, for an importation might come with
some new rose-bush from a distance. If you
are happy enough not to know them by
sight, let me say that they are little green
worm-like creatures—yet not quite a worm ;
working generally on the under side of the
green leaves (Mr. Henderson says that
one variety eats the whole leaf) ; and making your roses look as if they had been
through the fire. The fly is a small, gauzy-
winged busybody, with a black head. Neither of them can bear whale-oil soap ; which
for beings living on rose leaves, is not wonderful. Put a pound of this in eight gallons
of water, and syringe the bushes, or water
over the tops with a fine-rose watering pot,
just as the leaf buds begin to swell ; and repeat the dose two or three times, until the

7

leaves are full out. Then you will have no
trouble. Florists, of more experience than I,
say that *prevention* is the only thing with
slugs; and that if they once get on the bush
you can do little more. But I have not

MORNING GLORY IN SEED-LEAF.

found it so. Once or twice when I have
been away from home just at the critical
time, and so the early dosing was neglected,
and a few slugs made their appearance, I
have found that soap-suds and hand picking

together would even then effect a clearance.

During this month all seedlings may go into the open border, and all seeds be sown: some earlier, some later, according to their hardiness. Move those young things that

MORNING GLORY WITH FIRST LEAVES OUT.

are for transplanting as soon as they have a pair of real leaves, or are large enough to be handled easily; and thin out those that were sown at once in their summer home. It is hard to do this,—

one has such a feeling of the unknown
possibilities locked up in each inch of
green, and such a fear of pulling up the
very finest varieties where all look alike.
Yet this is sure, *unless* you thin them out (if
the plants have come up fairly) no variety
will do itself justice, and you will have a
patch of spindling, flowerless stems, instead
of abundant, thick-set leaves and blossoms.
Let your asters stand from six to twelve
inches apart, according to the kind, and
stocks twelve inches, and zinnias twenty.
Phlox may have a foot or more, according
to the soil, for that has much to do with its
growth, and alyssum and portulacca and
the other low half-trailers need but three
or four inches.   Sweet peas want no thin-
ning,—let them stand as thick as they will;
and mignonnette generally takes care of itself.   Then certain plants, like the tall
œnotheras and cockscombs, often show best
standing singly, one in a place, with no
other of the sort near by to divide attention.
Cannas always look best so (unless you

want a tropical bed on the lawn, filled only
with cannas and such like); and so do dahlias, and chrysanthemums, and tuberoses.
You get more good from the one alone, can
study and take it in better, than you can
with a group of three or six. But try experiments with a part of your flowers—experiments in grouping and bedding; prov-
ing their capabilities, and what suits your
soil and climate, and above all what suits
you; and then keep a record of your experience.

In warm quiet days, as the month goes
on and frosts disappear, plant out the tender
seedlings from your boxes; and turn out
potted plants into the border. Verbenas
may be risked among the first, and scarlet
geraniums I have always found to be of a
much-enduring disposition; and many tender things may go to the open air quite
early in May, if you are careful to cover
them slightly when the evening threatens
frost. Bell glasses are seldom seen in *our*
Fairyland. But a flower pot will do good

7*

service, and in quiet weather a cone-shaped twist of newspaper will be excellent protection from Jack's slight attacks; while a small box-frame with a bit of glass across

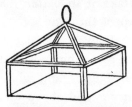

HOME-MADE HAND GLASS.

the top, can be left on both night and day in heavy weather. Or you may extemporize quite handsome covers thus: Get pieces of broken glass, of any variety of shapes; cut them or have them cut so as to fit a little; then join them, dome-fashion, with india rubber varnish and strips of tape. Varnish over the tape on the outside then, and fasten a wire or tape loop at the top for convenience in lifting.

Old baskets are good for the same purpose; and in England they make beautiful new wicker-work protectors. I am not sure whether it is much done here.

Mr. Henderson says, that any plants in pots which will be wanted for winter blooming, should be kept in pots through the summer; the hole in the bottom being well stopped up, that no roots may strike through, and the pots plunged—or set to the rim—in the open ground. The pots should be six or seven inches diameter in this case, so as to give the plant a little room.

But all others may be turned out to take care of themselves. Now if your potted plants have been repotted often enough, you will find the turning out very easy work. Lay your left hand across the top of the pot, letting the plant stem pass deftly between your fingers; turn the pot over, and strike lightly on the bottom with your other hand. This should be quite enough; and the little ball of earth and roots slips gently down into your left hand, the plant being steadied and held in place by your fingers. But if the roots have taken too firm hold of the pot to yield to such slight persuasion, then put a blunt stick through the hole in the bottom of the pot, and gently push against the crock that lies there. If both these fail, your plant has been long in need of repotting, and you must get it out the best way you can. "One proceeds with a knife, and inserts it all round the sides of the pot, and thus scoops it out; another favourite way is to break the sides of the pot with a hammer."* I have seen both these things done, and say to all my readers, Don't! And you had better lay the plant in water and *soak* it out, than with one great tug to tear it out by the roots.

Dig a hole in the border a little deeper than your ball of earth, and set the plant in a slight basin rather than on a slight hill. Fill up neatly, water gently and by degrees, —over tops and all, if there is not much sun upon the leaves. And in planting out, as in sowing, keep always in mind the general

* " Practical Floriculture."

effect as well as the individual display.
This, too, will take study and thought
and care. Your one rose geranium would
be lost among the grasses, and would
just smother the trailers, yet be perfectly
refreshing among the bright colours of taller
plants. Your one coleus or achyranthes,
so gorgeous in the sunlight, with a low setting of green or white, would lose half its
own beauty among shady monkshood and
full-faced perennial phloxes, without helping
them one bit. Notice even the style of leaf
and growth, as well as the colour of the
flower, in your arrangement; let the soft
feathery kinds have room to toss and wave
their tresses, and the sturdier ones shew all
the beauty of their strength in a tall background; and skilfully scatter those plants
which bloom but once among those which
are always in blossom, so that there may be
no bare, flowerless places in your beds at
any time.

I have been a good deal interested lately
in one of my seedling dahlias. Instead of

the two broad, full-fleshed seed leaves with which all the rest came forth into the light, this sent up one Siamese-twin of a leaf; the two seed-leaves that should have been, were joined together nearly their whole length, and with a single footstalk. Where would the true leaves make their appearance? There was no sheltering nest between the seed-leaves, but only an irregular, out-of-the-way affair, that looked as if it had never found out its vocation. I watched and waited ; the plant did not droop, it did not grow. The other young dahlias, its companions, put forth their first pair of leaves, and their second pair of leaves; and still the strange little seedling shewed nothing but its first one-sided growth. At last, when the third pair of leaves was unfolding on all the rest, the life in this began to stir. Down at the very foot of its one leaf stalk, close to the ground, came out a confused tuft of leaves. One seed-leaf—a sort of compound of what the first should have been and what it was—with a cluster of other and true leaves, as if first, second, and third had got all mixed up, and so came out in a hurry together. But once fairly aroused and in motion, the little plant kept on. And now, transplanted to the garden, you would not know it from the rest; unless, looking closer, you spied the shapeless little tuft that clothes the foot of the stem.

You will find, by this time, that the clusters of tulips and hyacinths, just past their beauty, are decidedly in the way; taking room that you want to occupy at once with other plants. I have seen it stated, somewhere, that if the roots are lifted carefully, and set in a trench in some reserve corner and well covered with earth, they will mature their leaves almost as well as if undisturbed. But I like "quite" much better than "almost," and have never tried this plan with any of mine. It seems to me that even if the old bulbs do not suffer, the young ones, just forming, must. A better way, I think, is to plant out your seedling stocks and asters and petunias among the

bulbs as they stand. By the time these little things have established themselves and
begun to grow, the others, whose work is
done, can be safely taken up. Look over
the beds from time to time, and wherever
you see a tuft of bulb leaves turning yellow
or dying off at the tips, that root is ready
for its rest. Take them up in dry weather,
and lay them in a dry shady place until the
leaves are quite dead. Label the different
kinds at first, and, when dry, store them
away in separate wraps of soft paper—old
seed bags are very good for this. Then
keep them in a dry, airy place until the time
for fall planting comes round again.

But you will say to me, many people
never take up their bulbs at all. I know;
but they lose a good deal for this little saving of trouble. The tulips and hyacinths
may bloom respectably for a season or two,
but they are sure to run down after awhile;
and your beautiful " King Pepin," or " Cicero," or " Duchess of Brunswick," instead
of one or two large, clearly-marked and

proudly-set blossoms, will give you a clump of most unworthy descendants. I believe this is even more true of hyacinths than of tulips. Besides, if they are left in the mixed flower beds all summer, they run much risk of being cut or injured by the planting of other things and the dressing of the ground. You cannot tell just where they are, and you cannot have a regiment of tall sticks to point them out. And labels standing alone are only pleasant in spring, when your beds are all promise.

Two ways I have seen described for making verbena beds, — both good, I suspect; certainly both worth trying. The first comes backed with a florist's authority : " To grow verbenas successfully, plant them in beds cut in the turf. Chop the turf well, and thoroughly mix with it a good share of well-decomposed stable manure ; never on any account plant them in old and worn-out garden soil, as they will most assuredly fail. Give them a change of soil each season, as they do not thrive well two years in

8

the same bed. Let the beds, if possible, be where they will have the sun the entire day. By following the above directions, one·may have a verbena bed that will be a mass of bloom the entire season."*

"I have two semicircular beds in which I have verbenas," writes "An Old Lady," in "Hearth and Home." "These beds are covered with bloom from the middle of June to the middle of October.

"Early in the spring, about the middle of March or first of April, I pull up all the old verbena vines, pile them and all the leaves they have collected round them in the middle of the beds and set fire to them, and when they are burned, rake the ashes well into the soil. A few shovelfuls of rich earth or well rotted manure is a good addition.

"About the first of May the verbenas begin to come up from their self-sown seeds, and when they are two or three inches high, I thin them out until they stand four inches

* Dexter Snow.

apart; they will grow very rapidly. As
soon as the blooms appear, all that are not
satisfactory are pulled up. The richest purple, the purest white, the most intense crimson, the softest lavender, and the rosiest
pink will delight your eyes; and there will
be no long, straggling stems or ugly patches
of burnt-up soil visible, but masses of colour and foliage, and material all summer
long for innumerable bouquets."

I have been obliged to shorten the pretty
account, but this is it in substance. Both
these ways are new to me,—the first comes
from Massachusetts, the second from Ohio.

Mr. Henderson, here in New York—or
rather in New Jersey—says, "Verbenas are
not at all particular about soil, provided it
is not water-soaked; we have planted them
on soils varying from almost pure sand to
heavy clay, and, provided it was enriched
with manure, there was but little difference
in growth or bloom." But *his* verbenas,
"set out in May, by August will have
spread to a distance of three feet."

So I am ready to think, after all, that the *care* is the thing. Not sod, nor soil, nor ashes; but cultivation.

One thing is sure,—verbenas should be well pegged down as they grow. Neat little metal pins can be bought, by the gross, for this purpose; but failing them, make for yourselves little crotch sticks with long ends and short top, such as you can cut from any brushy growth in the woods. Or (privately) use hair-pins! Petunias, too, thrive well under such confinement; and the trailing tropæolums or nasturtiums.

All sorts of training must be attended to now, when everything is making rapid growth ; for a little neglect at this stage of progress cannot always be set right by and by. If sweet peas once fairly try lying on the ground, they will lose much of their taste for climbing ; and an uncomely bend at this time of year, when plants are taking shape, may never be got rid of to the end. Have dark sticks (with the bark on is prettiest,—no painted sticks look half so well)

and plenty of soft strings. Twine and cord
are apt to cut; so if you have neither Japanese flax, nor bast mat, nor a yucca, take
old bits of worsted braid or binding; even
neatly cut strips of cloth will answer, only
let them be all dark coloured. Few things
look more forlorn in a garden than bits

STICK AND STRING SUPPORTS.

of red, white and blue rags, fluttering and
flaunting among the stately plants. Leave
no long ends of any sort; and cut leather
from an old shoe for the stronger shoots of
roses, etc., tying them with a cord passed
through each end.

8*

None of your gladiolus roots should be out of the ground much later than this. You may begin planting them by the middle of April (three inches deep), and may plant from time to time for several weeks; yet as the late plantings have most to fear from drought, I like the early work best. The different kinds will make a succession, even if planted together.

Remember that last year's tuberose roots (those that bloomed last year) will not bloom again; and so save both room and patience. Last year's *new* tubers or offsets, well cared for, will make blooming roots for next year, but not for this. In Italy, they say, where soil and climate are just the thing, the same tuberose blooms on from year to year, as the lily and gladiolus do with us. Here they give their white beauty but once. But how fair it is! How even superb, sometimes! I had a tuberose one year with a flower stem more than six feet high; and at the top a great head of sweetness, thick-set with blossoms, like a magni-

fied hyacinth; I never saw such another;
but even the small ones are delicious.

And so—

> "Like the swell of some sweet tune,
> May glides onward into June."

JUNE.

How vainly men themselves amaze,
To win the palm, the oak, or bays,—
And their incessant labours see
Crowned from some single herb or tree,
Whose short and narrow verged shade
Does prudently their toils upbraid,
While all the flowers and trees do close,
To weave the garlands of Repose.
—Andrew Marvel.

DO you find time, in this "high tide of
the year," to peep over your garden
fence now and then? taking a look into the
Fairyland which the Lord alone has planted? Have you kept watch of the progress
there?— from the first white saxifrage tuft
or willow catkin, down through all the wonders of squirrel-cup and wind-flower, columbine, arbutus, and Dutchman's breeches?
Have you seen the uvularia hang its delicate yellow bell? and found the May orchis,

(92)

rare every way in its fragrant pink dress?
Have your eyes rested on the white blood-
root, and rejoiced in the dog's-tooth violet?
with maple blossoms, red, yellow and green,
and tresses of birch and alder, and the white
clouds of shad blossoms, and dogwood in
fair array? Have you admired — afar off
and doubtfully — the great skunk-cabbage,
which has indeed the good sense not to
force itself into society, but comes out
when little else is abroad? And yet the
thing is extremely well connected, — with
plenty of handsome cousins, and some of
them in great demand. Your white calla
is one of these, and the rich golden-club;
and sweet flag — which many people call
"good enough to eat;" while midway between stands Jack-in-the-pulpit, handsome
and poisonous, like some other "incum-
bents" that might be named.

If you have followed all these in their
coming forth, then are you ready for the
June darlings. Wild lilies, in scarlet with
yellow linings; and partridge-berry, in

white velvet, perfumed beyond "the pow-
ders of the merchant;" and pliant hare-
bells, and the great yellow goblets of the
tulip-tree. Then you will not miss the
chick winter-green, with its striped leaf—
for "foliage plants" are not confined to the
garden; and you will watch for the superb
perfection of the wild lady's-slipper, or
cyprepedium.

Yet do not try to bring it into *your*
Fairyland. It will not live long,—it cannot
be itself while it lives. And this is strangely
true of many of our fairest wild plants.
Whether the dry, sophisticated garden soil
blights them; whether they pine for the
fresh scent of the woods, or miss their native shade; whatever it is, very few of
them are worth the transplanting. The
wild columbine loses its airy grace, and
stands up stiff and still in a large family
clump; the wind-flower thinks life not
worth the having; the little wood violets
lose heart when confronted with "czar"
and "king," and dwindle and wish them-

The Warner House &
Anna B Warner Memorial Garden
Constitution Island   West Point, N.Y.

selves at home. How can you comfort the partridge-berry, brought up in the shadow of the great pine woods? or what can make amends to epigæa for the loss of its free home among the rocks? Will tulips and hollyhocks be better society than the dear mosses among which they nestle?—will all *your* admiration make up for the song of the wild birds and the soft pat of the squirrel's feet?

There are some few exceptions to this, but in general (as I have found) it is among the hard stemmed plants. I have had the wild azalea live and bloom in its new setting, year after year; and the clethra, donning its white August dress as if at home. Yet they did not *grow* very much,—just lived and blossomed, biding their time. And in both cases I gave them a bed of their own native earth to rest in.

Then there is moss-pink. If you have ever seen moss-pink at home, revelling in the clefts of the rocks in the spray of the waterfall, I am not sure that you would much care to see it anywhere else; but, if not, you will find it a very Fairylandish thing indeed. And it is perfectly hardy, and does not need petting.

Talking of what we *may* transplant, brings us back, naturally enough, to what we may *not*,—the wonderful things that grow in the Fairyland of some other people. I have spoken before of the good effect of a bright-leaved coleus or achyranthus among the flowering plants here and there. And sometimes they may seem hard to get. I know all about that. But sometimes, too, a friend will furnish a cutting ; sometimes you may find one, not exactly "rolling up hill," as the children say, but still in unexpected places. *Not* in anybody's greenhouse, to begin with. *There* I would not pick up so much as a leaf from the floor. Professed gardeners are often very chary of their plants, even when their employers are not. Therefore take to yourself the old Arabic proverb, and " in a field of melons don't pull up your shoe." Yet, in other places, keep your eyes open. I have gathered seeds from refuse plants tossed over a garden wall on the Staten Island shore, and found a fine cactus cutting on the pavement in Broadway. And when times of sickness bring baskets of green-house beauty to your hands, then let the sweetness and the kindness take root and grow, in bits of myrtle and lavender and geranium, in small shoots of rare roses, or, perhaps, in the mere little fruit-stem of a cactus flower.

If your flower beds are at all far apart, or even separated, you will find it has a pleasant effect to divide the flowers as well—I do not mean in the way of mass-ing, but let the combinations be different. Do not have everything everywhere, ex-cept, indeed, those few rare things, like roses, without which no combination is quite complete. But let there be a natural system of surprises in your garden. Keep the heliotropes rather to one quarter, and let carnations have their special region of

9

bloom. Come upon the fuchsias suddenly, and let your tall perennial phloxes make a prospect in the distance. Chrysanthemums look best scattered, for at their time of glory they have the field almost alone; and the gladiolus and tuberose stems should lift themselves here and there in solitary beauty above the throng. So *I* think,—though gardeners say "three in a place" and "five in a place." Geraniums and verbenas may go anywhere and everywhere. But one likes to lose zinnias, and come upon balsams, and see cockscombs for a change.

In setting out little plants at this season, if the weather is very hot and dry, it is a good way to lay them—root and branch—in a pan of water, and so plant them all dripping out of that. Water gently and repeatedly then, rather than very much at once, and shade at noonday with cones of newspaper, or flower-pots, or bits of board and shingle, or a cabbage leaf on a stick. Flower-pot shelters should be raised a little at one edge,—the rest are airy enough.

Sow certain things for succession, such as alyssum and mignonnette; and if you can spare a bit of reserve ground, sow there small patches of many annuals, ready for emergencies. Keep back, also, a part of the little seedlings in boxes, for awhile, to replant in the borders; for your flowers will have disasters and enemies and disappointments, like the rest of the world. The shower that seemed certain to come, may go round; and the cool, cloudy day may turn hot and bright, withering the young plants to a very dangerous degree of faintness. Or, with this danger past, others may start up unexpectedly. Perhaps some wandering rabbit, surveying the world by moonlight, will be smitten with a desire to taste your one Japanese chrysanthemum, and will then and there cut it down to the ground, beyond hope of recovery—as happened to mine the other night. Perhaps some other night-walker, in whom the love of the beautiful has not been quite killed along with his moral sense, will covet and seize and bear away your very loveliest blue hyacinth, just then in its glory. Perhaps a brown grub or cut-worm, working away underground, will mow off a dahlia shoot here, and a fine seedling hedysarum there, with a few sweet peas and other trifles; making his night-meal of your most hopeful little plants, and leaving a mournful blank where yesterday stood the fresh young tuft of leaves.

Well, to him, at least, you can deal out justice. It is not easy to reach the other marauders—not even when the rabbit returns for a rose geranium and your first verbena blossoms; but the cut-worm can be found. He is hiding there close to the plant he has ruined; generally a little below the surface; waiting to rest himself and digest the chrysanthemum, before he marches off for a change of diet in China asters. I think in most courts, even in our day, his sentence would be :

"Guilty, and not recommended to mercy."

In all such cases, plant again, and do not

feel discouraged. There is only a limited number of cut-worms in the world, after all. I thought to myself this morning, when the whole garden was rejoicing over last night's rain, and only one of my poor stocks lay prostrate, that it was just the gentle tax we pay for the support of some of the Lord's creatures—creatures ugly to us, and yet having their appointed place and work in the world ; and probably (to a robin's eyes) their beauty. Of course, I would rather pay my tax in something besides gilliflowers ; and yet, after all, if it were left to me, what should I choose? A seedling heliotrope? a shoot of my new passion vine? a percentage of phlox? Should I offer Mr. Grüb a tuft of my thrifty mignonnette, fast pushing up into fragrance? Could I afford him part of my pansies? No, no, it is better as it is,—he breakfasting where he likes, and I seasoning my breakfast with patience ; for you know, though we might like to banish him to the garden behind the house, yet there would be serious inconvenience if he

9*

took to living wholly on melons and Lima beans. We don't welcome him, and when he comes we search him out with untiring zeal; but for the rest, we'll just replant and be content.

A few of your pot-plants,—geraniums, myrtle, and the like—may be safely detained in the house until quite late; both to repair such damages, and to replace hyacinths and tulips as they get out of the way. I rarely trouble myself to store crocuses and snowdrops through the summer. If you want them out of the beds, just make a little hole in lawn-turf near the house, drop in a crocus root—or a snowdrop—and cover it up; ànd so on, till they are all disposed of. They will sleep there, safe and quiet, till the time of the spring awakening; and then bloom out in full loveliness. So with snow-flakes and bluebells, or grape-hyacinths as they are called. I think they hardly ever show so well anywhere, as scattered about in the green grass.

If you have pot-plants that are large, you

may leave them in the pots and out of the ground all summer. Set them in the barren corners of steps and piazzas, letting them drape (if one may say so) the dreary hues and edges of boards and pillars. Or, if you set them out at all, merely plunge the pots to their full depth in the earth. In either case they need extra attention in dry weather.

POT FRAME.

And roses, as they grow, need frequent training and tying up. Those that send out long slender shoots show best when

trained as pillar roses; fastened rather
closely to a tall, strong stake, which should
be set as near as possible to the main stem
of the rose. Thus trained, the little short
flowering shoots will start out on every side,
and give you a pyramid or column of roses

very beautiful indeed. But be
careful to set the stake deep
and firm; else the first summer
gust may turn your pyramid
into a pink leaning tower of Pisa,
—not at all to be desired, and
hard to set straight. *Pio Nono*
is a fine pillar rose, and *Camille
de Rohan*, with its magnificent
buds and depth of color; and

FRAME FOR
ROSES, ETC.

Lamarque—white and exquisite; while the
Duchess of Sutherland is superb if allowed to
shape and train itself with the least help;
and *Salet* cannot be improved, and needs
only just support enough to hold up its
heavy head of sweetness. This last is a
" perpetual moss,"—lovely in every stage of
developement, and fragrant as an ideal rose.

Among the more tender kinds (all the above, except *Lamarque*, are perfectly hardy) you will find *Sombriel* very near perfection, and *Clara Sylvain* as dainty and delicate as its name, and *Camellia* and *Agrippina* an unfailing source of brilliant crimson and clear white blossoms, the season through. *Mme. Falcot* will give you plenty of lovely buff buds (the full-blown rose is not so fine) and *Douglass* is a rich deep red of peculiar shade and beauty. And to go back to the hardy hybrid perpetuals, do not fail to have *Jules Margottin* among your new roses, when they come.

All constant bloomers do best credit to their name if the faded roses are not allowed to remain on the bush. It is not enough to scatter the rose leaves in a pink and white shower upon the grass; the whole rose—calyx and seed-vessel and all—should be snapped off. Better still it is to take a small sharp knife, or pruning scissors, and cut back each flower stem that has lost its treasure, to a point *just above* the next leaf-bud. From this a new flower shoot will spring out, and your bushes will be in much more constant bloom. In this, or in any other pruning, cut clean and *short*, not with a long slant.

SHORT PRUNING.   SLANT PRUNING.

If anything has hindered your *preventing* the attack of the slugs, still wage war on them now. A few leaves may be injured and need clipping off; but whale-oil soap-suds will triumph in the end, and your roses come out all fresh and bright in the latter part of the season.

I planted at the back of some beds where a sort of screen was wanted, a row of gay vines—Ipomœa limbata, and I. kermesina, and the new bright yellow convolvulus, start-ing them first in the house. They grow

well, and promise to cover their rough cedar hedge with beauty. The browner, the
rougher your hedge sticks are, the prettier,
—so I think. A smooth green carpenter's
trellis never sets off the vines to so good effect. Let them wander a little on their way
to the top, and they will make all the fairer
show.

Flower beds now want daily inspection.
In spite of all your care some few seedlings
will die; so that one morning you will find
a blank in a patch of asters, and next day a
vacant place among your stocks, and your
regular lines of phlox will become irregular,
needing a few new recruits. Then close
watching against the weeds is of much importance, and far better than fighting against
them. Sorrel and clover and couch grass
will make short work with your delicate
plants; choking them, starving them to
death, making them die of both shade and
hunger. For so enwrapt with a coarser nature than its own, the seedling flower can
get strength from neither the ground nor

the air; can never drink in the dew nor
bathe itself in the sunshine. And weeds
have a fashion of starting up exactly where
your young plants are set; availing themselves of protection, it may be, against hoe
and rake, as an army sometimes advances
with prisoners at the front. Hoe and rake
are, indeed, of little use here; and only in-
exorable fingers can avail. Nor can these
always help making sad work, if the weed is
well grown and the flower very young. In
such a contingency (which may come up
sometimes, even in the best regulated gardens) put the fingers of your left hand close
about the stem of the little plant, holding it
well down, and then with the right hand
root out the weed, using a quiet, steady
pull, rather than violence. If the verbena
or aster can be thus kept in place, while
only the intruder is uprooted, it will probably soon establish itself again and grow
on joyously. But if the weed roots have so
wrapped it round that it must needs come
out too, then you can only replant and

water and shade. Take notice here to have your seedling plants *quite* clear from weeds when you set them out. Let them at least begin all right. Don't trust the innocent green faces of the seedling weeds that sprinkle the surface of the pot earth, pretty as they may look just now. Young chickweed and clover have a power of growing up that is quite astonishing to unsuspicious people.

I remember, as I write, that some great authority — Mr. Henderson, I think — says it is a shame ever to have a visible weed in your garden, — they should all be destroyed before they can be seen. And "true for ye !" — as some of the weed-pullers would say. There never would be a weed seen in *my* garden, if I had ten men at my disposal. Or ten women. But some of us cannot spend quite all our time in Fairyland.

When clipping off the dead roses, as I have advised, look over those that are just opening, to see what evil-doers may be there. Some rosebug, founding a colony ; some green " worm i' the bud," choosing for himself a pink house, which he will straightway turn into a ruin; some leaf-roller, perhaps, tying up the whole end of a young shoot for his own private apartments. If you will take a little trouble with these creatures in time, you never need have much to take.

I have paid heavy taxes this week. For two or three years past I had been trying to raise the climbing fumitory—*Adlumia cirrhosa*—from seed; and after many failures, last year one plant grew but did not flower. I kept it in the house all winter, not trusting the hardiness of so young a plant, and this spring set it out in the open border. Late frosts came, but did not hurt it; and soon new fresh leaves began to replace the faded winter tuft. Then the leaf shoots began to twine, elongating themselves curiously into a sort of tendril. I gave it the help of a bushy cedar stick, and up went my fumitory hand over hand, like Jack's bean with Jack after it. Presently the leading shoot was five feet long, and I began to watch for flower buds.

One morning, going out to attend to some other plants near by, I glanced towards my pretty vine, and saw that its delicate leaves were drooping. Not with the sunshine, alas! They were not faint — they were dying. And, yes; just as I thought; the whole vine was cut off at the very root! Not the leading shoot, merely, but every smaller one also, which might have taken its place. And, of course, close to the scene of destruction, barely hid away under the soil —too full to move, was the largest sort of a cut-worm; snugly curled round and reposing after his night's work. Judging from this one specimen, I should say that adlumias have a fattening quality which is quite remarkable.

VINE SUPPORT.

I left the root of my poor vine, to see if perchance another shoot would spring up ; but no, it had lost strength or courage. Then I took it up, and planted Thunbergias,—and didn't much care whether they grew or not !

But oh ! what rare Japanese pinks are blooming out now, and what heartsease ! And every night *Œnothera Lamarckiana* opens its lovely blossoms, and my seedling petunias are coming in all sorts of styles. White lily buds are pushing on apace, and Mr. Vick's *L. Thunbergianum grandiflorum* is opening its rich dark beauty, and Mr. Henderson's lobelia *Miss Murphy* wins general and loving admiration. The new pyrethrums that I raised last year from seed have been in bloom for weeks, in many tints,—not double, but very showy. The candytuft which I transplanted is in full bloom, and so is the self-sown mignonnette. And if you want a truly beautiful variegated geranium of the zonale class, get *Black Hawk*.

It is a time for the constant doing of little things, this flowery month of June. The grand spring planning is over, passing fast into results testing its excellence. So also with the spring planting—its bright anticipations, its many hopes. The days, as they roll on, say pleasantly: "*Nous avons changé tout cela !*" What is left? What has come out of it all?

To begin with, let me say that it is too soon yet for our gardens to be new editions, in many-coloured bindings, of "Great Expectations Realized." You must give even the most industrious and well-intentioned flowers time. Is it nothing, think you, to elaborate such wonderful tints and forms from the colourless air and the dull, brown earth? nothing, to arrange and perfect such a system of roots? nothing, to assimilate all that a plant can, of sunshine and rain and dew? How long does it take *you* to grow to perfection by that same process of (mental) assimilation?

Therefore do not try to hurry your plants

10*

too much,—give them every needed help, every delicate attention; and let them have time, and do you have patience. You must not expect to see your Fairyland what gardeners call a "mass of bloom" so early in the season. If the beds were full now, they would be over-crowded by and by; therefore enjoy the flowers that are out and the growth already made, and be thankful as well as patient. Cannot one wait a little among such troops of roses? Why, my *Souvenir Henry Clay* is so heavy with bloom that neither stake nor string will hold it. I have tied it again and again. *Pio Nono* is all in green just now, at the end of the month, gathering strength for a fresh outburst; and *Salet* bears the last few of its new crop. And the beautiful *Mme. Bosanquet* blushes always; and *Mme. Falcot* wears her daily dress of dainty buff; and *Mme. Plantier* has well-nigh said farewell until another year.

Just over *Mme. Falcot* rise the tall stems of my *excelsum* lily, with pendant bells of rosy buff, touched off with anthers of deep orange red. The annunciation lilies (L. candidum)— old, classical, but too pure or too something for most modern gardens— are sweet after their own rare fashion, gleaming out in spotless white ; and to my great pleasure, my new L. auratum shews three buds that promise full developement. The first one I planted, promised and failed. This was put in without any manure near it, and does better. L. thunbergianum and L. fulgidum are both past or passing, but both are fine : the first, a dark, gloomy red ; the second, red, flushed with orange.

You will think I have forgotten the little things to do, in the great things done.

First of all, then, there are weeds—always weeds—to be nipped long before they reach the bud. Then there are bare spots of earth between your plants, uncovered as yet, and always prone to bake and harden in the June sun. For both of these a small, fine rake is the best cure. Constant working among your plants, with a careful hand, is the greatest possible refreshment to them as well as to you. How easily the dew takes effect upon the softened earth; how surely some sweet and gentle influences find their way into your spirit, if the care-trodden routine of life is broken up and stirred by work among those things which God has made and not man.

JULY.

Canst thou bind the sweet influences of Pleiades, or loose the bands of Orion?

Canst thou lift up thy voice to the clouds, that abundance of waters may cover thee?—*Job* 38 : 31, 34.

I DO not know how any one can take full comfort in his garden who does not meet the Lord there. If all the little disappointments are to be borne alone ; if all the beauties that spring up under your hands bring no thought of the hand that created them, then the garden will be a very shorn place indeed, and you will fail to get from it half its richness. For the loss of a favourite plant makes us rich—and not poor—if it comes as a new, gentle lesson in learning the Lord's will, in accepting his choice instead of our own. That *acceptance* (it is more than mere submission) makes a thread of perfect gold all through the duskiest life-pattern.   And do I think it is in place with such very little things?   O yes!—with everything.   I had seen very little of life-work when the knowledge first came to me.

I was standing by the river side waiting for my father, who at that time went to town every morning and came home every night.   This night he failed to come.   I saw the little boat break through the river-shadows with her line of light, I heard the oars dip and work, but the seat in the stern was empty.

Dr. Skinner stood near me on the land-ing,—stepping about, musing, half whistling, as he often did Not talking to me, nor seeming to notice me just then at all.   Yet perhaps his eye caught my look, or his ear my tone, as I said quietly,—

' He has not come !"

With one of his quick motions Dr. Skinner faced round upon me.

"Are you resigned ?" he said.   That was all.

I have had greater things to resign since

then, but the lesson about little **things has** never passed away.

How do you manage in this July weather,—sometimes hot, sometimes dry, always uncertain? How do you get along, when "the dust groweth into hardness, and the clods cleave fast together," unless you recognize the Lord's hand in it all, and so accept his work? Easy then it is to wait for "the small rain, and the great rain of his strength;" easy even to bear "the treasures of the hail," if they come; well knowing that the "clouds are numbered in wisdom."

It is not an unmixed pleasure to go over your garden, even in the best of weather. Some blanks will be there, in spite of everything. For instance, this year asters and phlox and gilliflowers—three of my especial pets—have been in the dumps, and not disposed to grow. I planted them out when too small (don't do that), and then was obliged to leave them to look after themselves, (also not to be done, if you can help it).

Then I think the mischievous thrips, too small to trace save by their mischief; being (to quote Carlyle) " like grains of gunpowder—singly contemptible, but highly respectable in mass;" I think they have browsed upon my poor seedlings in preference to older plants. I have sowed both asters and phlox again, for replanting.

It is pretty to note the quickened progress of things, as the season gets fairly under way, and plants begin to realize that if they are to make a show at all, they must be about it. How fast the slender verbena widens out into a spread of beauty—in what a hurry the sweet peas come out; purple and white and painted ladies jostling each other with soft wings! Seedling petunias display their eccentricities, the last one open, having a large white blossom with a deep purple stain in the centre, as if one of my pansies were stationed there on guard. How fairly the geraniums unfold leaf after leaf, like a ship crowding sail as the breeze freshens! By the way, it was a little incautious in me, dealing as I profess to do with things attainable by everybody, to instance *Black Hawk* of all my geraniums. For that is a twelve-shilling novelty—one that I should not have had myself, but for the open hand of a great florist, who is as generous as he is skilful.

If you would keep your garden from degenerating into very seedy real life, as the summer goes on, you must keep all dead flowers picked off. Sweet peas, for instance, will bloom the season through, unless you let them ripen seed. *Then* the vines spend all their strength upon the swelling pods, and presently turn yellow at the root, and cease to be a thing of beauty or a joy. So with pinks, so with many other flowers. Some, indeed, take care of themselves. Petunias drop their blossoms and leave no sign that mars the plant, and pansies seem to have strength for everything; but verbenas and geraniums, though they go on blooming, yet soon get a sort of encumbered look if the seed-heads are left on. Of

course where the seed is ornamental, and
the plant grown chiefly for that, these words
do not apply. Honesty (lunaria) must not
be shorn of its dead flower stems, and the
ornamental gourds must be left to perfect
their fruit. But as a general thing you
never need fear to pick your flowers with
the greatest freedom; you will have all the
more left. It is the very way to make them
bloom, a friend of mine used to say; and
she was one famous both for picking and
having. It holds good in many depart-
ments, from the days of Bunyan down :

" There was a man (though some did count him mad),
  The more he cast away, the more he had."

And so while some plants—and people—
live a stinted, dry, bloomless life, others,
through constant imparting of their riches,
are all blossom and fragrance. " They shall
still bring forth fruit in old age ; they shall
be fat and flourishing."

You can if you choose leave a few pods
for seed, if you wish to save your own.

But generally enough will ripen in hiding
places, tucked away out of sight among the
foliage, to answer all your needs; and in the
case of sweet peas, the seed is so cheap
that even this is of little consequence.
Mignonnette seed you must gather from time
to time, choosing those capsules that shew
dark grains within their small open mouths.
And pansy seed you must watch for,—the
seed-vessels burst wide apart almost before
the seed is ripe, scattering it hopelessly.
Sweet peas have a trick of doing this, too;
and phlox, and balsams; and some people
recommend a little muslin bag tied round the
flower stem, for a seed-catcher.

In saving the seeds of asters and zinnias,
make sure that you go quite down to the
bottom of the chaffy cup in which they rest,
else you may get *only* chaff; and let all new-
gathered seed lie out in some airy shady
place to dry a little, before you put it away.

Whenever you can get ladies' small pruning shears or scissors, you will find them of
great use in all these clipping operations

For while they are strong enough, by means of a sliding spring, to cut easily a good stout shoot of old wood from a rose or a black-berry, they are also so small and light as to lie in a little basket and work in a tired hand. Such a pair can be found at the chief seed and agricultural stores, price from $2 50 up. Shears without the spring are cheaper, but will not do the same execution. Arrange a small plain basket, for work, not show; with your shears (or failing that, an old pair of scissors), a knife, half a dozen labels, a pencil, and some strands of bast mat, or other soft strings. Then in another basket, larger but still light, have a trowel, and support-sticks of various lengths, and you are equipped. The sticks should be smooth and straight, with the bark on if possible; and the labels neatly fashioned out of bits of old shingle, not less than four inches long. You can get these labels from the seedsmen, ready made, for twenty cents a hundred, if you can spare so much from your seed money. There is no better way of marking

labels indelibly (that I know) than the old
one :—whiten the smooth surface lightly with
white lead, and write while it is wet, with a
common pencil. If you have an indelible
garden pencil, the wood must be wet with
soda or saleratus water instead. Some people prepare a number of labels thus, and
so have them fit for use at any time.

And when the two baskets are ready, and
your day's work is done, then go forth together in the edge of the evening for rest. You
will forget how tired you are while you are
tying up the pinks, bowed down with only the
weight of their own loveliness. And the dry
cares and parching disappointments of the
day will somehow grow gentler as you sprinkle soft refreshment on the little seedlings
that have also, after their own fashion, been
bearing the burden and heat of the day. And
the pruning, severe though it may have been,
in your life experience, will somewhat
change its look as you catch a glimpse of
the needs-be, through the medium of your
own wise and tender meaning in what

11*

seems—at first sight—so harsh. Cut back
the roses? pinch out the balsam's leading
shoot? insist that your ipomeas shall climb
at your pleasure, instead of wandering aim-
lessly about? Ay,—and a few weeks will
shew why ; in the abundant colours and the
richer green, in the close, compact, *working*
growth. A few weeks for the flowers ; but
with us it is a few years. Even so.

"Every branch that beareth not fruit he
taketh away, and every branch that beareth
fruit he purgeth it, that it may bring forth
more fruit."

Among the hardy perennial flowers, there
are many lovely, old-fashioned kinds, well
worth the having—if you can get them.
Spiderwort, with its deep blue eyes; and
ragged robin, with its funny fresh look of
inconsequence, daffodils and rocket for the
early spring; and periwinkle and moneywort to carpet any bare spot of ground ;
and lilies of the valley, and Solomon's seal,
—with a host more. Some of them you
will find in the florist's catalogue; a few in

the seedsman's list; but everywhere under a
new name, where you must have sharp wit
to find them out. For few innocent mind-
ed persons would ever guess that Alyssum
saxatile meant golden basket, or that Lych-
nis flos-cuculi and ragged robin were one and
the same. It's all nonsense, by the way that,

" A rose by any other name would smell as sweet."

Can you get at the perfume of a wall-flow-
er through Cheiranthus cheiri ?

Well—have all of the old-fashioned beauties you can get and find room for; but
some I fear live only in memory, and many
have retreated to the gardens where fashion
never comes. There you may find them—
if you can find the gardens; and can may be
get a root or a layer or a " slip " for the ask-
ing. They will not all grow well from seed.

In these days, when there is so little to do
in the garden except waiting for rain, and
fighting the weeds that *won't* wait for it, the
spare minutes may be well employed in in-
creasing the number of your plants. Not

by sowing seeds—it is too early yet for that, except the few things that are sown for succession; but in the way of layering, budding and making cuttings. This last, Mr. Henderson calls the most important of all floral operations; furnishing, with care, an inexhaustible supply of plants. And he adds the comforting assurance, that care is the thing needed, not great knowledge. Yet a little knowledge is a good foundation for care's work.

When I was a child, I was taught elaborately how to make cuttings in the English fashion, by our English gardener,—a man thoroughly at home in the business from a seven years' apprenticeship and much use. His success was always good; and mine, following his directions, was rarely wanting. Yet some of these English ideas Mr. Henderson has, American like, cut down and simplified; and so I shall sometimes choose to give you his directions, rather than those which I could more properly call my own. The simpler the better, always.

Leaving for the present some varieties of
the work which are better suited to the cool
autumn months than to this dry heat, let
me tell you first what can be done now.
Layers can be made among your roses any
time from the middle of June, till the September frosts set in. The shoots should be
new wood, not more than a month old.

LAYER, SHOWING CUT, PEG, WEDGE, ETC.

Make your cut in the midst of the green,
fresh leaves; first down half through the
shoot, and then along, splitting it lengthwise

for three quarters of an inch or more, according to the size, and on the *upper* side. Bend
the shoot gently over, and peg it down, with
the cut an inch or so deep in the earth.
And it is usual to put a bit of stone or stick
—any small trifle—in the cut to keep it
open. The layers may be made in the mere
garden bed, or in small pots sunk up to their
rims by the side of the bush. Layers in
pots give the strongest plants *soon*, as they
can be set out in the fall with less disturbance to their roots, and so get better established before winter.

Another plan, very successful in hot
weather, is a sort of *air* layering. Did you
never notice a broken twig, which hanging
just by a mere fibre of bark, had hardened
and granulated at the broken end, as if all
ready to send out roots? I have,—and
wonder now at my own stupidity that could
not put two and two together. For that
was really an air layer,—only when made
on purpose, the branch is cut and wedged
open just as for an earth layer. The roots

will put forth into the mere open air; and then the layer should be at once cut off and set in a small pot, and shaded and watered until it begins to grow.

In making layers from some plants, the shoot is not cut, but is twisted—or has a bit of the bark taken off.

Budding, too, is summer work. Let it be done, says Mr. Henderson, either so early that the new shoots can ripen before frost, or so late that they will not start until spring. That is, either before midsummer or in the fall. The stem or stock on which you bud must be in just that state when the bark will easily quit the wood; and the bud itself must be taken from a well-grown shoot,

PREPARED BUD.

thus. Cut across the shoot a half inch or so above a leaf, and from that cross-cut bring the knife down through the wood to as far below the leaf, taking out a bit of bark and wood an inch long, and sloped to a point at the lower end, like a long, narrow

triangle. Carefully take out the bit of wood
from the bark and examine the bud at the
foot of the leaf, to see that it is sound and
perfect. If there is a little hole there instead, throw away your bit of bark and try
again. Then on the stock make a cross-cut

STOCK WITH INCISIONS. STOCK WITH BUD INSERTED.

just through the bark, and from the middle
of this a like cut straight down and as long
as your bud. Gently loosen and lift the
cut edges of bark, and slip in the point of
your bud, easing it down till the leaf stalk

is near the centre of the long cut. Then
bind it firmly round with bast-mat or lamp-
wick, winding the strand above and below
the bud, taking care not to injure that in
any way ; not letting the binding cover it,
nor making the whole so tight as to cut into
the bark of the stock. You merely want to
hold the bud in place, and to keep out the
air ; covering the cut edges of the bark com-
pletely, so as to give the stock and bud a
chance to unite.

STOCK AND BUD
BOUND UP.

For good buds of choice varieties, as well as for cuttings,
you must sometimes depend
upon friendly gardens having a
larger variety than your own.
And remember it is of first-rate
importance in budding, that
the bud should be plump and
fresh. Therefore if the bud
shoots are to be brought or
sent any distance, be careful
to guard them against even
the first symptom of dryness,

They may be packed in damp moss and oil-silk paper, and go safe ; but as people seldom carry those conveniences in their pocket, and as one may be offered a new rose-shoot when one is away at a tea-drinking, let me tell you a substitute.   Ask for a raw potato, cut it in two, and stick the ends of your rose-shoots well in.   There is nothing better. I am not sure that any of the books recommend a plan so unlike all " modern improvements," but our old gardener approved it greatly ; and he would go off in a hot morning and bring back a potato full of new cherry buds, or have apple shoots sent to him thus from a hundred miles away.

Hot weather is not the best time for *cuttings ;* but of course we who live by our wits must learn to make use of things just when they come, and cannot refuse sprigs of geranium because it is July. We get them in a bouquet, or on a visit; or they come to bless our sick-room. And here let me say, there is no sweeter kindness to an invalid than to send her flowers—cut flowers, not a dress bouquet; and there is no better amusement for her (if she can do any thing) than to play garden with them. A knife and scissors for trimming, a saucer of sand; water and sunshine; are all she needs for great success in striking her cuttings. Then fresh earth, a kitchen spoon, and the smallest sort of pots when they begin to grow. It is such fascination to study fresh life when you are languid!—life that is not flaunted in your face, that does not extinguish you with its wild breath; but is gentle, quiet, tender, with the very fragrance of the Lord's touch. Sitting there by your flower-stand, with eyes shut or open, there comes over your restlessness a certain sense of rest, and peace somehow soothes away even the thought of discontent.

" The earth is satisfied with the fruit of Thy works."

And as we remember, we are satisfied too.

When by any good, honest means we have cuttings of fine plants at our disposal, then comes the question what to do with them, how to make them grow? The way is not hard. But first about getting them. Do you think I am needlessly fastidious? Where a plant is large, why may not one take a cutting? Or what harm to gather from another plant, loaded with ripe seed? That sounds reasonable; but it does not work well. An unmanageable golden rule encircles other people's flowers, to my eyes: a sure sense that, for some reason or other, *somebody* would rather I should not touch. Perhaps those seeds are the very first that have ripened, and the owner has not yet secured her own supply — perhaps you might take off a cutting in just the wrong place. One thing is certain: if you know a person well enough to treat her plants as if they were your own, you also know her well enough to ask leave.

Now then for our cuttings. How will you choose them?—if you can choose,—for upon the proper ripeness of the wood will depend much of your success. In all soft-wooded plants, such as fuchsias and verbenas, the shoot should be so tender that it will *break*. Where it *bends* under your fingers, the wood is already too hard to furnish the best cuttings. They might grow, but neither so soon nor so vigorously. In roses and other plants called hard-wooded, the shoot may be somewhat riper. It is difficult to give an exact rule—try, and learn.

Then make your cuttings short. From two to four inches is quite long enough, and even a single inch is worth much, even in non-professional hands. *Professional* ones will almost strike cuttings from the shadow of one plant and the smell of another. But you will need to practise a good deal before you can divide a leaf and get a plant from each end.

Make a smooth, clean cut across your shoot, just below a joint, say the old gardening rules ; but it seems now that this is not needful with most plants. " Blind shoots"—*i. e.*, shoots with no flower-bud at the end—are the best in roses, and perhaps in other plants. Clip off a few lower leaves,

12*

and set your cuttings pretty close together
in three or four inches of sand or earth,
covering them up to the first joint. Press
the earth firmly round them, water tho-

CUTTING AS SET OUT.

roughly, and then never allow them to
wilt; giving also plenty of air but not
much sun at first.

With the "saucer system"—grand for dry
weather or a sick room—you set the cuttings in a common saucer full of common

sand ; then keep them in the fullest sunshine you can find, and also keep the sand
as wet as very wet mud. In either case,
pot off the cuttings in small separate pots
of fresh earth as soon as they begin to push

CUTTING AS SET OUT.

out new leaves,—sure sign of growth begun
at the root end. Shade them for a few days
after potting, and keep changing into larger
and larger pots (just one size larger each
time) as fast as the roots begin to crowd
out of the hole at the bottom of the pot, de-

manding more room. For quick success, and strong, thrifty young plants, I have never tried anything so sure as the saucer of sand.

Another plan which I have found good for roses—and have seen used for oleanders and other hard-stemmed plants—is to fill a common phial with water, put the cutting in an inch or so deep, and then tie a string round the neck of the phial and hang it up in the warmest, sunniest place you have. This is a good variety for sick-room gardening. I have a little rose-bush now — one of the *very* finest in my garden — that during its cutting-life hung for weeks in the sunshine at my window, while I sat in the shade.

Cactus cuttings need a treatment of their own. The least bit will grow, even the green fruit below the flower; but before planting, lay them by in a dry place for a week or two to let them wilt a little. If planted at once, in their full succulence, they may decay. Let the pot be well drain-

ed with cinders—you may fill it half full if
you will—and let the earth on top have a
good mixture of sand; and give little or no
water till the cuttings begin to grow.

Most plants will grow from cuttings of
their shoots,—others as well, or better, from
cuttings of their roots. You know how the
long underground stems of your roses,
which go wandering round and rooting as
they go—you know how full they are of buds,
every one ready to shoot up and become a
stem? You may take one of these ram-
bling roots, cut it up into little bits an inch
long, each with "eyes" like a potato set;
and then opening a shallow drill in some
undisturbed, unoccupied place, you may
sow your root-cuttings as if they were
beans. Cover lightly, water them, let them
alone, and they will grow to your heart's
content. Bouvardias strike better so than
from cuttings of their shoots; and so does
the sweet-scented shrub (Calycanthus) and
many other plants. It is a good way to
raise rose stocks for budding. A *difficult*

cutting is more sure to grow if struck under glass; and we who have not sashes nor bell glasses, can use instead a cracked tumbler or a finger bowl. For *our* Fairyland is only in results.

Florists often prepare for their cuttings beforehand, by so trimming the stock plants that they will throw out a quantity of the right sort of shoots. For instance, with the verbena, Mr. Henderson advises this: " In August, cut back the old plants about six inches, fork up the soil and give it a dressing of fresh compost; then, by October, there will be plenty of first-rate new shoots, just fit for cuttings." But it is rarely needful to do this in any small, private garden, for one seldom wishes many plants of any single variety, and so enough good cuttings can be found without special pains to provide them.

If you have not the money to buy cheap statues — poor plaster figures of men and beasts — to set about your grounds, be thankful: there is no Fairyland within *their* shadow. But if you want to beautify an

unmanageable old stump, or put a spot of
colour in some rough corner where few
things will grow, the way is easy. A basket stuffed with moss; a tea-chest adorned

MOSS BASKET.

with pine cones or a tracery of old rope,
will fill very creditably either sphere. They
must be fastened securely in place, filled
with good earth, and stocked (not *over*-
stocked) with plants. Moneywort, periwinkle, ivy, or an ivy geranium, to trail
over the sides; or failing these, nasturtiums,
thunbergias, even petunias will do. Verbenas are always pretty, and lobelias always
in place. Stone-crop is fine and useful too,

helping to cover the ground between taller plants. In short, take what you have—here as elsewhere—and make the most of it. For a basket two feet across, Mr. Henderson directs seven upright plants — large and small — *Mrs. Pollock* geranium being the centre ; then seven drooping ones. And he says the basket should be lined an inch deep with moss to keep the water from washing through.

RUSTIC BOX.

AUGUST.

I hear the blackbird in the corn,
　The locust in the haying;
And, like the fabled hunter's horn,
　Old tunes my heart is playing.
　　　　　　　　　　　—*Whittier.*

THE vacuum which—according to the popular saying —" Nature abhors," certainly never shews its dreary blank in our Fairyland. Things change, softly,— and the appearance of things : hyacinths go out and lilies come in, and then annuals come crowding up to fill the ranks. Tall perennials too look down upon the *new* people,—beautiful phlox heads, waving their abundant bloom in the fresh wind; and lark-spur, blue-eyed and dignified; and monks-hood and fox-glove. Cassia Marylandica— a wild native beauty—will thrive and flower without stint, if transplanted to your gar-den ; needing plenty of room and giving in return plenty of handsome yellow flowers. Sweet day-lilies bloom too, in these shortening August days; and grasses come into flower; and locusts and grasshoppers sing of the time of year.

As fast as your gladiolus spikes pass out of bloom, cut them off, leaving the foliage untouched to ripen the roots. Happily for us, we need not sigh for the " novelties " at two and five dollars apiece. Twenty, and thirty, and thirty-five cents, will give what ought to content reasonable people. *Canary*—a grand bloomer, early; with a fine spike of large flowers of a beautiful buffish yellow. *John Bull*—very large, creamy white. *Mons. Vinchon*, of a fine pale salmon tint. *Berenice*, another first-class,—spike rather open, flowers very large, colour a rosy salmon. The new *Isabella* (it was quite new when Mr. Vick sent it to me) is more wonderful for its spike than for the individual flowers which it bears so grandly, though they are very fine too,—clear white, blazed with purple. Then there is *Don*

Juan, and *Fanny Rouget*, and *Imperatrice*, and many more; costing little and paying much.

My seedling dahlias come finely into bloom, despite the dry weather. The first one that came out, of the bouquet section, will I think be quite double as it gains strength. The next, large velvety crimson, is but semi-double, yet very showy. The third, dark red of the brick cast of colour, is as full and round and double as a dahlia can possibly be. Another has come out in bright clear yellow, and there are purple-tinted buds on the next. Certainly growing dahlias from seed is a great idea. My packet of seed cost just ten cents; and I have had the pleasure of raising and watching them, and now (if one may judge by the beginning) they will make a grand show. And a certain amount of pure *show* in a garden is useful,—helping to conceal the blanks, helping to bridge over the intervals between one set of loved flowers and another. One does not *love* dahlias:

but I have come nearer to it with these seedlings than with any I ever had. And they do their best.

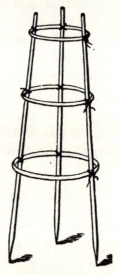

DAHLIA RINGS.

I believe it is one of the characteristics of Fairyland, that things start up in unexpected ways and places. One does not expect to pluck kindness from a frozen geranium, nor to have interest and sympathy

spring up in the place of a slain fumitory;
and yet in Fairyland such things will happen. And I could almost pardon that grub
(were he alive) that destroyed my one adlumia some weeks ago, for the kindly letter
of promise and the generous supply of new
plants, which have come to me from different quarters. I think a flower garden (that
one attends to oneself) does scatter other
seeds, of yet sweeter things, in one's own
heart! The owners of such gardens always
seem to have the old motto in the child's
story,—

"Whatever we possess, becomes doubly
valuable when we are so happy as to share
it with another."

And even some of the florists who sell
their treasures for money, cannot help
throwing in what Mr. Henderson gravely
calls "a few extras," for love. And so my
garden breathes out all sorts of sweets,—of
kindness among the rest. Here are roses
and geraniums I never ordered; here are
seedling plants of some annual "novelty"

13*

which I thought I could not afford, and Mr. Vick somehow thought he *could*.

Asters need careful staking and tying up —the slender sorts—as they grow taller and begin to send out their buds. Put the stake close to the stem of the plant, firmly down, and let the end and upper part of it be hid in the leaves and shoots so far as may be. Never try to fasten several branches with the same string; they will always be crowded and look ill. Some kinds of asters are called strong enough to stand alone; but summer gusts are very trying, and blown-down plants are very forlorn.

For balsams Mr. Vick recommends some training and trimming, as well as tying. For instance, pinch off all the side shoots, and the plant will grow into a tall straight cylinder of blossoms. Or for a change of effect, leave three or four side shoots, and pinch out the centre one. Either will make a beautiful show; or if you prefer a more natural growth and shape, the balsams from Mr. Vick's seed are large enough and bril-

liant enough to bear all the pretty leafage
that comes with them. But in a large garden it is well to use all sorts of different
ways, to give a look of freshness and variety, and break up any approach to stiffness.

When you have plenty of room, some of
the finer daturas may well be allowed a
place. D. Wrightii and D. humilis flava fl.
pl. have hardly a fault, save their belong-
ing to a bad family. You must start them
early to have them bloom the first year.

Œnothera Lamarckiana should have a
place—more than one, I think—in every garden, notwithstanding its long name. It is the
fairest thing at night-fall, and in the moonlight, and until the sun gets hot next day.
Call it evening primrose, and let the rest
of its titles go; but it is a great improve-
ment on the older flowers of that name.
Its rapidly, softly opening buds are bewitch-
ing, and you will find all your guests drawn
to the primrose quarter after tea, almost as
regularly as the evening comes.

Among the beauties just now in bloom, are some of the delicate lobelias,—the blue L. gracilis, and L. erinus—white-eyed, and the little new L. *Miss Murphy*. This last is like a soft green cushion, starred over with white. So it holds on its beautiful way—dropping its old blossoms with no mar, and putting forth the new with no failure—always dressed in the same exquisite white and green. It is said to be every bit as good for pot or basket culture, as for the open garden.

Another pretty tuft—wonderfully pretty considering its family—is the little French marigold, *Tagetes signata pumila*. A single plant in a place,—some place where you go for general effect and not sweet companionship and greeting, does excellent service.

I am quite fond of the dwarf convolvulus (C. minor) with its honest blue eyes and eager endeavour to do its best. A sleepy little plant—that is the worst of it; much given to long summer-day naps; but in the cool fall weather it grows wakeful and bright.

Portulaccas too are not mid-day flowers; much as they love an open, sunny situation, and well as they stand dry weather, their blaze of beauty cannot bear the direct heat. They are all aglow at breakfast, and nowhere at dinner. Poor soil agrees with them, and a mixture of lime rubbish improves their colour.

For gay steady bloomers through heat and drought, few things are better than the dwarf tropæolums — T. minor. How brilliantly T. King of Tom Thumbs faces the withering sunbeams, and comes off with flying colours! It quite refreshes one even to see such endurance. How rich in contrast are the dark maroon blossoms of T. King Theodore,—not black, as was said at first— (and now, in some unscrupulous catalogues—) but very, very dark. One of the deep worsted-shades of red. Mr. Vick says the finer climbing tropæolums make a beautiful bed, if well pegged down; but I have never tried them so myself.

There's a temptation to everything just

now to run wild and look weedy. The well-established position, with roots deep down and heads far up; the easy, prosperous circumstances; with frequent showers, and the warm August sun and the cool August dews—is it wonderful that even flowers should slightly lose their wits and their sense of propriety? Petunias run about, embracing everybody, and mignonnette gives itself up to the pleasure of living, and my passion-vine is clearly seeking for more worlds to conquer. Little reck they of an aster cut down last night; or of a fuchsia torn from its place by a wandering dog, to make room for his huge stolen bone; or of white little Miss Murphy, well-nigh turned out of house and home by the same process. Do they care that one tuft of phlox hangs its head in a dry corner; or that my pansies dwindle and grow faint in the sun? Do they cheer on the little modest *Silver Queen* geranium, patiently putting forth one fair leaf at a time, as it gains strength? Not a bit. And so my Fairy-

land of flowers has one thing in common
with the gay world of Newport and Sara-
toga. But did you ever notice, that when
people choose to be like each other, it is
often in just those points where they might
much better be different?

In some of the dry, hot times of weather
that come now and then,—indeed in almost
any weather that checks the growth of your
plants,—there is a certain small unseen
enemy that does great mischief—the blue
aphis. Perhaps you may wonder how—if
he is not to be seen—I can know that he is
blue,—alas! he is visible enough, only not on
the surface. Look under ground and you
shall find him, to your heart's great discontent. Has it happened to you to have some
pet verbena or heliotrope suddenly stop
sending up shoot after shoot with its crown
of blossoms, and take to listless gazing at
the more active world around it. You
water, and shade, and coax—no use. There
the plant stands, insensible,—not dying, yet
hardly living. It is a case where there is

little danger of doing harm, therefore dig
up the plant, mid-summer though it may be,
and examine the roots. The first thing that
strikes you, perhaps, as you begin to stir the
earth, will be a crowd of ants,—hurrying,
scudding along, and bearing off countless
white eggs to a safer place where there is
no earthquake. And with much indigna-
tion you charge the failing health of your
poor heliotrope upon *them*. Quite a mistake : the ants are innocent. Look further,
—take up your plant bodily and examine
the roots ; and you will see that they are
covered thick with minute specks—or clusters of specks—of a dull mealy blue : this
is the blue aphis,—one of the worst of all
the garden pests, and the hardest to deal
with when found. Mr. Henderson says the
best chance of cure, is to water the plant
for a week with tobacco water, " about the
colour of strong tea." I have succeeded
by taking up the plant and patiently clear-
ing it, root by root, of its enemies. Then,
especially if transplanted to a new place,

there is good hope that your pet will begin
to grow again. But I am rarely troubled
with the blue aphis. If ever another case
comes to my hands, I shall try washing off
the roots with whale-oil soap-suds.

It is time, even now in August, to begin
to think of winter flowers for the house,—
deciding what we have room for, and what
we want. Some are to be raised from seed,
and some from cuttings, and others are to
be pruned or repotted or taken up. It is
too early of course for the general taking
up of tender plants. Let them enjoy their
freedom while they can, and make the most
of out-door advantages for a month to come.
But in seasons of dry weather, which do
come now and then, I have tried a very successful plan with certain plants that have
rather given way to the season,— neither
making much show nor holding forth any
hope of it. They are just living along till
better times, with roots all quiet and tops
that make no growth. Now in this slum-
berous state a plant will feel removal much

14

less than when it is in full wakeful vigour.
Choose your opportunity, make calculations
about the time.   Is it likely that this small
fuchsia, or geranium, or heliotrope, will
start so suddenly and grow so fast as in any
way to distinguish itself before you are
close upon frost?   If not, I counsel this :
Have good compost ready, and fresh clean
pots (they can be soaked and scrubbed out
when foul); then take up your listless plants,
pot them carefully, water them well, and
place them in an airy porch or piazza ; or
if you like, after a few days shading, just
plunge them in the very beds where they
were before.   The fresh earth, the free supply of water, give the plant a start instead
of a check; and it will perhaps not drop a
leaf, but just begin to grow and bloom and
look lovely ; and then it is all ready for removal to the house at the approach of frost.
Of course if the weather is dry, you must
keep the pots well watered, wherever they
are.

If other plants that were turned out or

plunged in the spring, have grown straggling
and bare, cut them in ; that the new growth
may be well begun before repotting time
comes. It is bad to give a plant everything
to do at once.

As the season passes on, and flowers suc-
ceed each other, take note of any perennials
that are ill-placed, so that they may be removed in the fall. And if different mem-
bers of the same family have got in a confused state, without due regard to height
and colour and contrast, label them carefully now while they are in bloom. It
is very hard to remember in the spring
which small green tuft bore crimson heads
last summer, and which bore white,—
whether the tall striped *Triomphe de Twickle*
stood here, or only the low-growing, pink-
eyed *Marie le Croix*. Therefore mark them
all now.

I am convinced that it is well, where
you can, to have a bit of reserve ground,
with a stock of reserve flowers always
ready for replanting. Late-sown asters

and phlox and balsams—that is *very* late—
do not always thrive ; but you can remove
quite a large plant from your reserve
ground, taking it with a good spadeful of
earth to a hole already dug in some blank
place in the borders, and with very little
disturbance to the roots. If the plants in
the reserve are kept thinned out and cared
for, so as to be strong and stout, this is easy.
Then the borders can be always full, and
one will not have too many petunias—
which happened to me this year. I was
glad to let anything cover the ground
where grubs had been so busy.

I have said so much about growing *patience*—perhaps you will think I need recommend no other " common things." Let joy
and admiration—gay tropicals that live only
in the sunshine—have it all to themselves.
But there will be shady corners in your
Fairyland ; and while patience makes some
of them lovely, let meekness make others
all sweet.

Meekness among the flowers ?—yes, you

will want it. For you must know that criticism there is much what it is elsewhere, and "best efforts" meet with only their common reward. You will find the one weak spot in your garden detected, the one failure noticed before the many successes. What has come from necessity will be laid to your choice, and your spare minutes must bear the blame for not doing the work of hours. People who have not tried, know so much of gardening !—and so little. But bear it all meekly,—much of it is true—on the face. There *are* too many petunias, no matter how they came. And the young weeds you have been trying to get at for the last week, are still in sight. And some plants do not flourish—a painful fact enough, without your being asked reprovingly— " What is the matter with them ?" Some people " would give half" your stock " for carnations"—as you would perhaps, if you had the money ; and some " don't like zin- nias"—useful as they are when you cannot afford a background from the tropics ; and

14*

others "would peg down the verbenas"—
as you would, if you could get a minute's
time. In one's garden as in the world, one
must learn to be content; even when the
blooming successes are passed by, and the
failures picked out; wearing there, as elsewhere, "the ornament of a meek and quiet
spirit, which in the sight of God is of great
price."

Photo by W. H. Stockbridge

ANNA B. WARNER

SEPTEMBER.

"Who loves a garden, loves a greenhouse too."—*Cowper.*

THERE is a certain quickening of everything in these fall days,

"When suns grow meek, and the meek suns grow brief."

The flowers are in utter haste to make the most of themselves, and to show what they *can* do; and you, half wondering why they could not have tried a little harder all summer, instead of waiting till they were on the very confines of frost, watch their fall perfection with an enjoyment that is partly sad. Not much to be done for them now— not long can they do anything for you. But with the happy sequence of things in this world, there are the winter flowers already needing your attention.

Many of the simple border annuals will

bloom well in the house; and the little self-sown seedlings of these that spring up here and there in the beds, make extremely nice plants, if taken up and potted before they get too large. Turn back the edges of your tufts of ageratum, and you will find a thrifty set of young ones,—easy to transplant, and sure to grow. So with sweet alyssum, and candytuft, and pinks; but mignonnette does not like handling, and generally grows best if sown directly in the pot. Portulaccas may be taken up just before frost, the large plants; and if carefully potted will blossom in the house for months. Make cuttings of any favorite petunias and verbenas, and also of geraniums: the newly-rooted plants will give more leafage and better chance of house-flowers, than the old.

Foremost among winter flowers, for beauty and brilliancy and certainty of success, stand the bulbs; and yet they are very little grown by people in general. Florists have them in plenty, and great private green-houses have them, a few; but the small pri-

vate sitting-rooms and sunny windows of
plain, quiet dwellings, shew almost anything else. Geraniums, oleanders, myrtles,
pittosporums, hydrangeas ; old - fashioned
fuchsias, never promoted beyond their original name of " ear-drop ;" roses — more
bush than bloom ; even a prickly cactus or
two,—all these you will find grouped together. Growing as they best may in boxes,
pitchers, unwholesome glazed flower-pots ;
furnishing " slips " now and then for a visi-
ter, but loved by the owner more for the
care they cost, and the hard struggle their
life seems to be, (often so like her own,) than
for any return that life can ever hope to
make. I know she comes to have a sort of
tender regard for even the little bare twigs
and leafless sprays that one by one give up
the struggle and must be clipped off. It is
hard to gather them up and fling them into
the fire. They bore up against adversity so
long,—so long lived on without the sunshine, so many times were nipped by frost
or parched with drought, or withered with

the stove's fierce heat. When did any one
of them have fresh earth? Not within the
memory of the oldest inhabitant of that
flower stand!

But among all this varied assortment, how
rarely do you find anything like a bulb.
Callas are there sometimes,—now and then
a stray amaryllis; but tulips and hyacinths
almost never. No gentle snowdrop, indoors
or out, to ring in the spring with its green-
tipped bells; no gay little crocus, nor graceful scilla, nor tall polyanthus narcissus.
To all of these I want to call your attention.
And the fall is their planting time.

Not quite yet, of course, — even when
August has given the last one of her beautiful days, it is still too soon. I am not
going to talk of the planting just now, but
only of the choosing and buying.

Bulbs are not dear, to begin with. Of
course you can find lilies for five dollars a-
piece, and expensive novelties of all sorts;
but tulips in general range from ten to thirty cents apiece; hyacinths, from twenty-

five or thirty to eighty; narcissus, from five
to fifty. Named crocuses are forty cents a
dozen, and snowdrops still less. If you do
not care about knowing your flowers as in-
dividuals, and so can dispense with the
names, you will save yet more, but lose
some pleasure. Names are a great deal to
me, but many people care nothing about
them. Yet how could I properly describe
Tuba Flora, so that you would not get it all
mixed up with *Penelope*, if they had no
names? How could you order *Fanny Kemble*, and run no risk of getting *Pigeon* instead? No disrespect to that most estim-
able little crocus; but *Fanny Kemble* is one
that even the great pleasure-giver herself
might be willing to have bear her name.
Why, one comes to a sort of personal familiar acquaintance with *King Pepin* and the
Duchess of Parma, and *Dorothea Blanche;*
instead of their being only " the great white
tulip marked with red," and "the smaller
white tulip marked with less red," and "the
other tulip " that is just a strange glory of

red and yellow. I think names are a great institution, myself, if they do cost a little.

But here, as with the seeds, you need a catalogue. There is so much more pleasure in choosing for oneself, than in taking anybody else's selection. You can get rather more for the money by leaving it all to your florist ; but you lose the fun—and fun is a great thing. And there is even less danger of mistakes among the bulbs than among the seeds ; for there are few difficult ones, and almost no shy bloomers. Bulbs expect to do their duty and make a show, under all circumstances.

The catalogues of seeds and roots for fall planting are just beginning to come out. Mr. Vick's is already in hand ; and is about as bewildering (for its size) as his list of seeds. The first thing then, is to clear up and arrange your own ideas. Read over the catalogue till you are tolerably familiar with its contents,—till " blush white," and " pure white," and " dark blue," and " porcelain blue," and " rose," and " red," begin

to convey some distinct vision to your
mind. See which names, which descriptions,
attract you most; for curiously enough,
few as the words are, and unknown the
names, they do attract—and attract differ-
ently. "*Ami du cœur*, tall," is quite another
thing, you feel at once, from "*Bleu mourant*,
late, low." Pass back and forth through
this wilderness, then, until you in a measure
know the way. After that, settle your business questions.

First, how much to spend. Second, what
proportion of your bulbs shall be for winter
blooming in the house, and what for spring
blooming out of doors.

Next, see how many tulips can weigh
down one hyacinth, and whether a lily can
outweigh them both. Can you get *one* of
the more costly things? Can you divert a
little from the humbler and less costly?
Hard questions to answer, I know well.
The persuasive power of rival beauties has
been a trouble from the days of Paris
down.

Let me say for your comfort, with a *good* catalogue in your hands, you can hardly go wrong. Take one that is prepared by an honest and reliable man, and you will be almost sure to go right. For the dearest things are not always the finest; and a ten-cent *Standard royal* may be just as true a "novelty" to *you*, as a one-dollar *King Pepin*, or any other new beauty that has taken its place and price. If I could only give you some faint idea of the wonders that decked my garden last spring, you would see that these same mazes of the catalogue are no desert land.

Concerning varieties of these fair winter flowers, there must after all be differences of opinion, as about other things; and to really advise, therefore, might be—on the whole—to disappoint. I shall counsel nothing, but that you choose for yourselves. This being distinctly understood, I can with a clear conscience go on to tell you of some things I have especially enjoyed.

I have said that bulbs are reliable,—yet

they will not *all* bloom, any more than all
your seeds will come up, or all your cuttings grow. Some crocus or other will take
a distaste to the world after seeing an inch
of it, and so droop down and fade away.
Some snowdrop, rising higher to peer out
through the window panes, will discover
that after all it is not spring ; and in your
warm room its white buds will turn yellow
and shrivel up with disappointment. Some
enterprising tulip will run so fast, going all
to top, that there is nothing for it but to
tumble down and die ingloriously of mere
want of root and patience. Such things
will be in this typical world of flowers.
And thus you come to look at the successful ones, the finished specimens of flower-
hood, with a certain added gladness and ap-
preciation. They have fully wrought out
the beautiful plan of their life; there are no
more failures possible for them.

Snowdrops, when they do well, are parti-
cularly lovely in the house; their pure
white and green tinting seems like a very

bit of imprisoned spring. And the scillas might be the spring sky, and the crocuses the spring sunshine — that is, the yellow ones. Anything more exquisite than my crocus *Gold Lac* last winter, could not be imagined of the sort. Six bright gold blossoms, striped and dashed and touched with the richest dark brown, came up like fairy-rockets—two together, three together, one alone. And all from one small bulb. *Fanny Kemble*, on the other hand, following slowly and with dignified steps, was of a beauty hard to describe: the shape, the whiteness, the purple marking must be seen.

Sir Walter Scott is another grand crocus, —*very* large, beautifully striped.

Do not try to grow the large show tulips in the house, but take instead the little *Duc Van Thols*,—pretty sure to do well, *very* sure to give pleasure. Especially (just this one bit of counsel) the rose-colored,—have that by all means. The bud comes up quite white.

"*That* will never be a rose-colored tulip," said my sister, watching it from her seat by the fire. But as the days went on, the little white tulip began to blush. It could hardly be (in this age of the world) for being looked at; but blush it did; and the sweet rosy colour grew and spread and deepened, till my tulip was all warm and flushed like a child awaked from sleep.

Little *gold-striped* Van Thol is very good too,—bright and sonsy and "peart," as our freedmen say.

Slowly, while all this goes on (it is last winter, in my study, you understand), a blue *La Perouse* hyacinth has lifted its head from the brown soil and the green leaves; and now as one waxy bell after another takes colour and shape, you ask if there was ever anything quite so fair? Yes, *Lord Anson* follows, bating no jot of his rosy pretensions; and the white *Emieus*, and the pale yellow *Pluie d'Or*, lose nothing by having to follow instead of to lead.

I do not generally plant my finest bulbs

15*

for the house, nor often the *new* ones; but some of those that have already bloomed in the garden, or young offsets. For pot or glass culture is said to weaken the bulb; and people who get but few new ones each year cannot afford that. I like to see them first in their full glory out of doors. But such roots as I have mentioned—not new, nor quite full-sized, give exquisite flowers; though of course the spike is not so large.

Then for another house beauty, have at least one polyanthus narcissus,— nothing can be much pleasanter inside your window, when the snow lies deep without. Even a little simple narcissus—such as *Incomparable* —brings its yellow cup absolutely full of the spring.

Then anemones and ranunculus. And for them, I must say they are uncertain; they may bloom, they may not. If everything is just right, they will; if everything is not, they won't. That is about the state of the case. But *if* they bloom, they 'll make you so happy that you will go on planting them

every year for the mere chance. I had a
pot of ranunculus in bloom one winter, that
fairly brought people in from the street.
Such balls of colour! such violet perfume!—
the only flowers, I think, that I ever knew
smell just like a violet. And as for the ane-
mone, she is a queen!—whether she wears
her robe of scarlet, or of purple, or of deep-
est violet blue.

It is hardly fair to speak of jonquils after
these. Yet they are both delicate and dainty, and well repay one's care. And some of
the oxalis tribe yield great returns; and
cyclamens are exquisite and expensive;
and the amaryllis is doubly ditto, ditto; and
ixias, and many more are to be grown, if
you have room, money, or opportunity.

So much for house favourites.

Out of doors, I may as well confess at
once that I have too many favourites to name
them all. You would grow tired, if I did
not. I must name a few, and then deal only
in general remarks.

If your crocuses and blue-bells are scat-

tered about in the grass, then, to bear them
company, plant a few Persian iris in the
beds,—close at the front, for they are low,—
with a little clump of Bulbocodium vernum,
to give another variety of colour. They
will all be up very early.

Then come the hyacinths—rising higher
and higher as these first light troops of blossoms clear away, and going steadily on to
their perfect bloom, regardless of frost or
even snow.   There is the white pyramid of
Semiramis, and the lovely *Duchess of Bedford*, and *Belle Esther*—her white dress picked out with green. There is *Triomphe Blan-
dina*, the great waxy bells in a flush of
beauty ; and *Penelope*, suffused with a mere
thought of pink.

Princess Royal wears her rose colour in two
shades ; and *Eendragt* has flowers like a
star ; and *Tuba Flora* one knows and names,
even at a distance, so large, so beautiful.
Norma, too is in the group, and the *Duchess
of Richmond*.

There stands *Othello*, as dark as he knows

how, being only a hyacinth; surrounded with the softer tints of *Mimosa* and *Charles Dickens* and *Nimrod;* and these in turn with *Blocksberg, Richard Steele, Envoyé,* and *Grand Vedette.* There are the yellow *Louis d'Or* and *Piet Hein* among the doubles; with the deep-hued beauty, *Rhinoceros,* and *Pluie d' Or* and its shower of pale gold. Neither must I forget my pet, *La Cherie*—the blue-eyed white lady that comes almost last of all, shunning the crowd.

When these exquisite tufts of clear pink and white and yellow and purplish blue (true blue is the rarest thing among flowers) have graced your borders and gladdened your heart for a while, suddenly, some morning, there comes a change. Off among or beyond blues and pinks appears a spot of brilliant red, a streak of flame colour,— and there is tulip *Brutus* open to the sun. *Claremont Gold Lac* follows close, and *La Reine* and the *Grand Duke of Russia* are not far behind. The garden has been full of love and beauty; but now some dash and

enterprise and display, — robes of purple,
and great cups of gold, and banners of
every shade of red. Even the *Marriage de
ma fille* is a marriage in high life, and the
Bride of Haarlem is clearly "a lass wi' a
tocher." How they "fall in," as the soldiers
say, donning their colours in hot haste. The
purple-striped *Caiman*, and *Yellow Prince*,
and *Couleur Cardinal. Dorothea Blanche* holds
her ground modestly, as some people will,
in a white dress and pink cheeks; and *King
Pepin* is royal in his markings. How superb
is the *Duchess of Parma*, in *her* court dress;
and *Rose Gris de Lin* and *Proserpine*, are like
two roses for colour, and *Lac von Rijn* quite
lovely in its quiet lilac and white. In general, I think the single tulips are much the
finest,—much more like tulips, and one pre-
fers to have a flower look like itself; yet
there are great beauties among the doubles,
with over-skirts extremely rich and *bouf-
fants*. Besides some that I have named,
Incarnat Gris de Lin and *Conqueror* could
hardly be improved.

Then there are the parrot tulips — gay, rich, almost flaunting—yet not quite; with cups too large to be held up; and last of all, the Show Tulips, as the florists call them; late, tall, and of more regular beauty than most of the early kinds. No one who buys *Cicero*, or the *Duchess of Brunswick*, will think his money ill spent.

Next in order of blooming, are my favourite hardy gladioluses (I follow "Agriculturist" authority in my plural)—by no means to be compared with the late-flowering French hybrids, and yet giving wonderfully pretty bloom, and plenty of it, long before their French cousins begin their toilet. Plant them in the autumn, and take the benefit of their cheapness. You can get them for eight or ten cents apiece.

Lilies come next, and they too should be planted in the fall.

But here I bethink me of my promise not to mention everything: remembering too that there are still left some things which I ought not to pass by.

Iris, with its rich peculiar blossoms; and Crown Imperial—gay but not sweet; and the little Anomatheca cruenta, and all the rest of your catalogue!

Get everything you can, and especially all the lilies; and make sure that you have at least one of the old *Lilium candidum.* So old that it is rare; sweet, elegant, spotless: worth dollars to you, though but fifteen cents to the florist.

Between the time when your list is finished, and with a sigh of relief that tells how great the perplexity has been you make a fair copy of the order and send it off, changing the possible into the inevitable,—between that time and the delicious minute when the bulbs arrive, each wrapped in its own soft labelled paper, and the "inevitable" order is changed back again into a box full of wonderful possibilities — to begin once more—between those two bits of time there is much to do. Of course you will question now and then with yourself, as to whether the box may arrive "to-day;" but, mean-

time you will not forget that there are other
things in the world besides bulbs. Do you
want columbines for next year, or hollyhocks, or fox-glove, carnations, sweet wil-
liam, or perennial poppies? Then sow them
now. These should all be planted early, for
if the young seedlings are not well established before winter, they will surely winter-
kill. For larkspur and some other hardy
annuals, it is enough if the seeds are in the
ground any time before very cold weather.
They will lie over till spring. Of course it
may happen, that all your seeds for fall sowing are in the bulb box—another reason for
ordering that early.

16

OCTOBER.

" He hath made everything beautiful in his time."
—ECCLES. 3 : 11.

THIS is so true, and the ever recurring freshness of the beauty is so new, so varied, that we are in a state of perpetual wonder as if we had never seen it all before. This sky is not the sky of June, but one look into its intense blue makes you content with the change; and the river is dancing with sparkles and flecked with joyous white ; and the wind—

" Ay, thou art welcome, Heaven's delicious breath,
When woods begin to wear the crimson leaf.

This by day,—but there come other things by night. Have everything ready, so that you can remove tender plants into the house at a moment's notice ; when some

(182)

crispiness of the evening air tells of frost.
Hardy plants that may yet need winter
protection, need nothing now. The later
they are covered, the better ; for they might
as well be frozen as smothered, and smothered they will assuredly be if covered too
early. The end of November is time enough
for that.

But make all preparations now, of every
kind. Gather the leaves as they fall into
some secure corner; pile up your brush
near at hand, and prepare soil and pots and
labels. Make all your fall sowings in the
reserve ground if possible, instead of the
regular beds. Most of the seedlings are
easily transplanted, and the beds are left
free for the late or early digging — late
and early, if you can give it—which is so
important to the summer display. One of
my beds suffered sadly this year in the dry
weather, because, being full of bulbs, it had
but a slight spring dressing ; and so the
ground hardened and dried as it never
should. For this same reason, it is well,

where you can, to have certain beds just set apart for bulbs; and them you can keep back some of your pot plants to fill them up when the bulb flowers have passed away.

For planting the bulbs you need only a good garden soil, well enriched with very rotten manure from the cow-yard, and softened and lightened with sand and leaf-mould if it is too stiff. It is also very important that the bed should be well drained; therefore never on any account plant bulbs or tubers where the water will stand at any time.

The same sort of soil may be used for bulbs in pots; though if you want the very *best* results (according to Mr. Henderson), you should make for them a compost of decayed turfy loam, river sand, rotted manure and leaf-mould, well mixed together. Mr. Vick says where the soil is stiff, it is well to give each separate bulb a little bed of pure sand to rest in. But we are not come to the planting yet; only I would say, have all your materials ready. The soil and the

sand and the pots; the boxes, if they are to
go in boxes; the moss, if they are to be
planted in moss. Shall I go further, and say,
the turnip, if—? "No; I most earnestly
hope that everybody who has a turnip will
put it to a more fitting use. Fancy content-
ing oneself with a hollowed-out turnip or
carrot for a hanging-basket, while there was
a yard of wire to be bought for two cents,
or a handful of moss to be had for the gathering, or an old box in the world that one
could cover with pine cones and bark! If
the ready-made pretty things are not attainable, set your wits to work and make
still prettier. The stems of wild grape
vines are fine twisting material, and bits of
old hollow branches, or old knot-holes with
their frame-work, may be cut and trimmed
and fashioned into the daintiest bulb-hold-
ers. Look about you in your walks,—gather conch shells by the seashore, if your path
lies there; or build up smaller shells and
bright-hued pebbles into handsome con-
glomerates of what shape you like. Then
16*

exercise your taste in suiting the bulb to the setting. Let nothing too elaborate spoil the simple beauty of crocuses and snowdrops; and give tulips a holder which shall be dark and rich rather than gay. I believe, for me, there is nothing so pleasant as the plain red flower-pot, with its fresh brown earth, for any house plant,—making no pretensions, it seems to accomplish the more; yet I have enjoyed a hyacinth in a glass very much, and some of the new crocus glasses are extremely pretty. As for porcupines, and beehives, and all the other enormities to which crocuses are sometimes condemned, I think they are just—worse than turnips! Could I say more?

As soon as your dahlia stalks are touched with the frost, cut them down; and either take up the roots at once, or leave them (some say) to ripen for a week. Store them in dry sand, and keep them dry and warm. Not in a *hot* place, of course, but more than just above freezing; and so with your gladiolus roots. Take up the cannas rather ear-

ly, for too much frost on their leaves is said
to affect the root, and store them also in
sand. Cannas will winter well in a good
dry cellar, but tuberoses do best with the
dahlias and gladioluses. Not the *old* tuberose roots, remember; but the offsets, which
will grow to a flowering size in two seasons.
Datura roots too may be kept in sand.
Most of the varieties are too tender for the
winter outside.

As the days turn cool, and the hope of
open air results grows less and less, secure
all you can to vary the colour and fragrance
among your window plants. Stocks that
have not yet bloomed will flower well in
the house; and a tardy young balsam, potted and trained to a single stem, will be
very handsome. So with some of the
dwarf chrysanthemums, — though they
should be left till the last minute. Try all
sorts of experiments,—but try them carefully, and note the results. Excellent discov-
eries are made in just this way.

Another thing is to be noted just now.

For tnose whose garden-room—and some other things too—is limited, it is very important to have especially those flowers that bloom all the time. In a great place, if a whole flower bed is out of bloom you hardly notice it, for the many that are *in*. But with us it is not so. Notice, therefore, as the season flies along, what blossoms accompany it, what others are scattered in its flight. Not everything will bear the frosts and cool winds even of October, and those that do are very precious.

First here, as elsewhere, come the roses—small Washingtons in their way, and everywhere taking the lead; in sunshine, in cloud, in loving favour. Yet not *all* the roses. *Ludovic Careau* has long been flowerless, and *Pio Nono* shows not even a bud, and *Camille de Rohan* reserves its brilliance for the glow of summer days. But just look at my perpetual moss *Salet*. Two or three exquisite full-bloom roses, as pink as June and almost as sweet, with large scattered buds here and there, as yet muffled in their mossy calyx. *Agrippina*, the brilliant little Bengal, offers both buds and blossoms with calm unvarying regularity, very regardless of weather; and *Mme. Bosanquet's* paler face is seldom absent. *Hermosa*, too, shows deep spots of colour. Now look at *Sombriel.* Long new shoots, thick set with their deep green leaves; and bearing high in air a perfect array of buds, in every stage of growth, and two open roses. But oh! such roses! Translucent white, into which there has somehow crept a thought of colour— *what* colour, you cannot tell. The whole so waxy and pure and moulded, that you are ready to repeat the comical remark once made by a greenhouse visitor, and say they are "just like artificial flowers." These do look "just like wax," only with a differ- ence, — the difference between life and death, the false and the true. Take one of *Sombriel's* breaths of fragrance, and you will debate the wax question no longer.

A beauty of another style is *Souvenir de Malmaison* with buds that are absolutely huge; three, four, and five of them crowning the stalk, disdaining any mingling with mere green leaves. And this great pink cup, almost as regular as porcelain ones and well nigh as deep, what is it like? What, but a Malmaison rose? The clear pink hue, the assured air of a queen; the dainty, coquettish air of a rose,—it is a superb flush and blood beauty. Not etherial, not *spirituelle*, like *Sombriel*, the *Malmaison* has never learned—and does not believe—that

> " Il faut souffrir, pour être belle."

There is nothing like roses, even for October. I have counted (some years ago, when my garden was better filled than it is just now) two hundred roses in their perfection, on my own bushes, at one time,—and that time an October morning. And this did not include the over-blown roses, nor the half-open buds.

Coming down from these heights, it is pleasant to see how many of the intrinsically fine things, of humbler pretensions, yet

hold their own. Mignonnette, always lovely
and always sure, now outdoes itself; and
sweet alyssum makes a small white wilderness that is very sweet indeed. And pinks
show white stars, and crimson stars, and
stars of all shades; and verbenas bloom
steadily on. Pansies take breath after the
summer heats, and look out upon the cool-
ing world with wide open eyes and expan-
sive faces.

There is a sort of sadness in the late
bloom of the less hardy things,—the tuberoses, dahlias, and zinnias, which are so gay
to-day and may be cut down to-night. One
turns from them to the chrysanthemums, just
coming out, defying the frost. Ah, Grub!—
if you had only not eaten up my one Japanese specimen last spring! However, Mr.
Vick's wise counsel to rejoice over the flowers that live, rather than to mourn over those
that die, is strictly in place here. Have I
not *Gloria Mundi*, already answering to its
name; and *Eve*, softly opening out its paler
tints; with *Dr. Brook's* gay orange, and *Ful-*

gidum's deep red, and *Snowball's* perfect white. I have seen this last loaded with its beautifully incurved, globe-shaped blossoms, and these in turn bearing a spotless weight of early snow, themselves almost as feathery and white. Chrysanthemums are just grand whenever the season is long enough to give them a chance. They thrive better, I think, for a light covering of brush or leaves during the winter months : not that they are not quite hardy ; but this seems to secure an early start in the spring, and for plants that may be called to a neck-and-neck race with the frost, an early start is very desirable.

Among faithful, sure bloomers at this season, I must not forget my lovely Louicera Halliana : perfectly hardy, a cloud of white sweetness in the early season, and from then until now never without a good show of its graceful blossoms. I got one two or three years ago from Mr. B. M. Watson (who I believe first introduced it in this country), and have had constant comfort in it ever since.

When your bulbs arrive, choose out first those that are to be for winter pleasure indoors. These must be first planted. And if you have others of your own, from last year, it is well to look them over carefully, and set aside such as already show starting roots or shoots. These are early kinds, and will probably give early flowers in the house.

You may grow these pretty things in almost any way, and "with gratifying results." So florists will tell you, and they ought to know. Hyacinths, crocuses, snowdrops, scillas, narcissus, will consent to live and flourish in anything, for a single winter. You may take moss, or sand, or earth, or water; you may use (it is not always *choose*) a flower-pot or an earthen bowl, a glass, a wire basket, an old box, or a noseless pitcher; and (if certain other conditions are met) your bulb will do its duty and rise superior to all surrounding circumstances. But remember that moss and sand must be kept moist, with even

17

more care than earth; and earth must be light and rich; and the water in your bulb glasses must be always sweet and fresh. Not by changing it every week, as some direct, which is needless trouble and endangers the long roots; only sprinkle the water at first (after the glass is filled) with fine powdered charcoal. It will slowly settle to the bottom of the glass, in an unnoticeable thin layer, and the water will never grow impure. All you have to do, is to add a little more from time to time.

All florists (I believe) say that dark glasses are the best, giving the roots a shadow at least of their natural seclusion. Fill the glasses with soft water up to the neck, just so high that the bulb can touch it, and no more.

Planting in moss or sand I have never tried, having a strange fancy for seeing the bulbs in as natural a state as possible; but the authorities give this simple direction: If you plant in a bowl or vase having no drainage hole at the bottom, cleanse the

moss well before planting: if a common
flower-pot is used, this is not needful. Lay
the moss lightly in, arrange your bulbs as
you wish, and cover with more moss.

Sand (sea-sand) must be washed to get
rid of the salt; and river sand should be
dried in the oven, to kill all animal life that
may be there. The tiny shell fish of our
river shore, will sometimes try the taste of
land plants if they have a chance. Some
planters mask the surface of the sand with
moss, after the bulbs are in; others like the
contrast of the green leaves and silvery
soil. But however you plant, the earth or
moss or sand must be thoroughly watered
at once; and then the pots and boxes and
glasses must be set away in a cool dark
room or cellar, where there is neither frost,
nor sunshine, nor mice.

Florists generally advise the planting of
several bulbs in the same pot. I can only
say that with me it does not work well.
One will bloom, and another will lan-
guish,— three gay tulips, and one dying

or dead,—two snowdrops up, and the third refusing to follow; or one crocus in bud, and the other quite past its prime. If they are in separate pots, the failures can be removed, and the rest closed in to hide the blank. Even for a great window-box I think I should put all the bulbs in pots. But of course that is a matter of fancy.

If you have no good place in the house for your bulbs at first, set a large box or open frame in the garden, on a dry walk or a bed of coal ashes, place your pots on this, and fill in between them with coal ashes or tan. Then cover the frame with boards, or spread several inches of dry leaves, sand, or tan over the pots. Frost will not reach them for a long time here, and in ordinary seasons they need not be stirred before the middle of November.

If you are impatient, and set your bulbs at once in the light, insisting that they should enact Young America, and bloom before taking root, do you know what you will have? Something about as valuable as a basket of neglected onions, with slim green shoots a foot long !

All, or almost all, advice about flowers, must be received with a certain degree of caution and mixed with a few grains of good sense before using. Fifty miles off, the middle of October is quite another time of year from our October 15th; and a wet clay soil, and a dry sandy one, make changes of season and condition that must by no means be disregarded. While one place is revelling in the golden glory of the fall, another is already fast in the chains of winter; and the late weeks of November, which find my garden in perfect working order, in another region come down upon an unmanageable wilderness of wet or frozen clay. It is true we prepare the soil for our bulbs, helping them to forget these differences as far as may be. But if *we* forget them, there will be failures of some sort.

A writer in one of the late papers says: " The earlier bulbs are planted in this month (October) the better." Now this is not al-

17*

ways true. You must study your climate. They should be planted in time to have a good root-growth before cold weather, but not so early that the green shoot will begin to push its way; nor so they will be up too soon in the spring, before the covering can be safely taken off. You do not want your beauties working their way through the leaf blanket, and hanging their pretty heads beneath the weight of driving snow. The last of October, or early November, are my planting times here on the Hudson; and from September to December are the extreme limits in all winter-having places. But take notice, the bulbs *must* be planted in some part of that time; you cannot wait till spring. Florists say, that orders are sent for tulips and hyacinths just when they are ready to bloom! You must plant in the fall, with few exceptions. It is so hard for any but a practiced florist, having all facilities, to keep safely such kinds as may be kept for spring planting, that ordinary people had better not try. Lilies grow mouldy,

and anemones dry away to powder; all that
you cannot plant this fall, let a florist keep
for you till spring. If you cannot get
them, you will at least not lose your money.

It is strange work to plant bulbs. Beautiful work, but strange; having a certain
weird significance and likeness to greater
things. Seeds are another matter. A few
days, a week or two at most, brings up
their fresh growth; and even in this uncertain world we do all look ahead so far as
that. It is the gentle time of year, too,
when everything is tending towards sunshine and blossom and fruit. They are but
spring ventures. But for our bulbs!—Summer is behind them when they are planted,
and before them stretch the long, long wintry months of ice and snow,—the months of
absent or tuneless birds, of half-hardy things
that are dying, and tender things that are
quite dead. The very year is fading when
they are laid for their quiet sleep.

The seeds spring up and grow we know
not how; so swiftly, so suddenly, with

such a full burst of life. But the bulbs once planted, lying inches deep beyond the sun-light, lie still and give no sign. The labels set here and there in the fresh smooth earth, might each one bear the inscription: "Wait."

How long? And whose eyes shall see the bed in its glory, when the winter is over and gone? We know not. And so as I plant my bulbs, planning and mapping out, laying them carefully each in its place, there come through my heart these words:

"Who shall live when God doeth this?"

I cannot tell. But of that other resurrec-tion I know; though the waiting be long and desolate and wintry; I shall not miss the glory of that spring. "For them which sleep in Jesus will God bring with him."

NOVEMBER.

Our leaves are shaken from the tree,
    And hopes laid low,
That after our spring nurslings, we
    May long to go.
                    —*Gerald Massey.*

" A CHRISTIAN," says some old quaint
writer, "must be very careful to
keep his spirits up when his condition in
the world goes down." The words came
to me this morning, when I thought of the
present condition of things in my Fairyland.
There is no time, the season through, when
the garden should take such heed to its
personal appearance as now. The spring
promise makes you forget much; the summer fulness makes you overlook more.
Even the blankness of winter brings its ex-
cuse, for what can you expect then? But
the fall is a time of struggle and change

and new relations, which may be very rich, or will be very desolate.

Leave it to itself; let the weeds flourish and the flowers blow down; let the frost-bitten plants lean hopelessly upon their hardier neighbours, and the fallen leaves cover the ground with their damp mat; and your garden will be dreary with the forlornness of unblessed sorrow. Loss and disappointment and death have taken so much, let them even have the whole!—

Ah that is a wonderful mistake, in either case.

Look around, and see what the frost has spared. Make the most of it, cherish it. Gather away the wreck and rubbish of dead associations and useless regrets; especially unearth the weeds—those "roots of bitterness" which spring up but to trouble and defile. Remove with a smooth clean cut the broken branches, the hanging shreds of summer glory; clip off the dry flowers that blossomed when so much else was fair; and look bravely at the ground which God has cleared. There is always work for you to do.

It is astonishing how much can be done,— what transformations spring up under the wise hand of the fall gardener. Whole beds of mignonette, that were choked with decaying leaves, shine out and bloom with more than summer fragrance. Late roses, blown from their support, and trailing their delicate buds in soil and ruin, once lifted up and bound securely, shew tear-washed faces as lovely as any June-kissed darling of them all.

The heartsease revels in the cooler, fresher winds, with eyes so large and happy and quiet, that you cannot even miss the gay gladiolus and the dainty tuberose that once lived near by. And though zinnias are withered, and balsams are brown, and a hundred little beauties of the summer are sent into long, cold exile, yet there are white wreaths on the honeysuckle, and a few glowing pinks, while chrysanthemums are in their glory. How strong they look!

how warm in their bright colours! Even
the pale and white-robed ones lift up brave
faces to the wind. And if there is a sigh
and a thought in your heart for the more
delicate spring blossoms, that decked the
world

"When feelings were young and the world was new,"

still give thanks for these; for the glory of
work and character and endurance, when
the flush and promise of first things has
passed away.

You will find it sweet work to make the
most of these late beauties; training them
up, displaying them to the sun. For chrysanthemums, one or two barrel hoops, rest-
ing on crotched sticks, make a very good
support. Have hoops enough, and then
let the flower stems lie loosely and at
ease. They should not be tied up stiffly,
with stems bound close together so as to
crowd the flowers.

In the house, keep all your potted plants
as cool as possible. They have but just

come from the fresh air, and may easily
"get a headache" — as Dr. Kane and
some other people used to tent life have
done, when first obliged to sleep indoors
again.

There are something less than a thousand
and one ways recommended for the planting of your hardy bulbs. In ribband lines
of different colours; in separate clumps
of one; in regular one, two, three order,
wherein red, yellow, blue and white follow
each other without even a chance of escape:
all these and many more are directed, advised, and practised. A general helter-
skelter style finds favour with some, and also
the expensive fashion of having whole beds
filled with a single colour and a single name.
This may do well in great places, but I confess I should think the passed *Ami du Cœur*
bed would look mournful, with the *La Cher-
ies* not yet in bud. However, where ways
are so many, and opinions so countless, it is
a doubtful matter to put forth one's own.
Indeed for the great bulb owners, who have

18

everything and can do anything, I have nothing to say. If they can plant *Tuba Flora* broadcast, and have a half acre of named crocuses, and an avenue of Lilium auratum, they may be safely left to their own devices. But we, with just a handful of beauties, how shall we dispose them to the best advantage?

I will tell you some rules that have wrought fine effects in my own garden.

First, not planting too many together. For it is not a mere grand sweep of colour that we small florists want, but to study and enjoy the special individual plant. Not broad waves and stripes of tinted glory, a part of the great whole of our country seat; but groups of lovely, fragrant tufts and bells, each one a friend, each known by sight; making home more like home, and helping with their quiet grace to soothe and hush and charm away the small rough-nesses and weary breaths that come in the course of one's everyday life. A few hyacinths together will do this far better than a crowd. Therefore plant in small groups.

But next, make your groups different. Have no stiff arrangement of colours, yet *have* an arrangement. You will find a grouping of pink and white hyacinths quite delicious in its harmony and contrast; while the dark blues go excellently well with the pale yellow and lemon tints. The reds and paler blues are rich together; or the medium blues with the blush whites; and so on. You will find work enough for your fancy, if you give it a chance.

It rarely has a good effect to mix different sorts of bulbs in the same clump. The beauty of tulips, for instance, is so unlike that of hyacinths that they just put each other out. You lose the clear tints of the one, and the gay, dashing hues of the other. Snowdrops are too pale to stand among crocuses, and the Persian iris gets small credit for its lovely markings, if planted near the deep blue scilla or the bright purple bulbocodium. Give each sort a setting of space and brown earth, if you can ; and then you may pass from group to group with ever new refreshment and delight.

Another thing must be borne in mind. Some of your hyacinths are " tall," others " low ;" some are marked " early," and some bloom late. Now you want to have the clumps always symmetrical and shapely; therefore study the placing of your bulbs from this new point of view. If all the early ones are at one side, if all the tall ones are in front, it is easy to see that the effect will not be good. I generally give the matter a good deal of study.

When the ground is all prepared, and planting day has come, choose from your basket the bulbs for your first clump, and lay them out in order upon the bed — if hyacinths, six or eight inches apart, and tulips a little less, and crocuses not more than three. Then consider the arrangement, keeping each bulb in its labelled wrapper until you are ready to plant. And

as fast as you plant each one, set by it a
wood label with the name. Hyacinths
should be set at least four inches deep, lilies
somewhat more—say five or six ; and smaller
bulbs somewhat less. Two inches is depth
enough for a crocus. Lilies (the hardy
ones) should be placed where they can be
left several years without stirring, and crocuses and snowdrops will also thrive best
to be let alone. Tulips and hyacinths do
better taken up.

As the frost will sometimes throw out
your labels, and as it is also possible that
some of them may be raked off with the
covering of the bed in spring, I have found
it save trouble to make a sort of map of
each bed and group ; numbering each bulb
on my list, and writing down the numbers
in their proper place on my map ; so that
if a label is missing, I shall still know
what bulb was planted in that place.
Until you have learned to know all
your pets by name, it is a very good
way. After planting, smooth the earth

18*

neatly down, but put no covering on as yet.

I see it said by some advisers that it is not worth while to try to save your own bulbs. Take the good of them this year, then throw them away and buy more, for they will never be good for anything again. This is a mistake. Tuberoses indeed will not bloom a second season, unless in their beloved Italian climate; but all other bulbs that I have ever tried will live and flower admirably from year to year. If any of them see fit to abdicate at the summer's end, they always leave a successor so like themselves that you cannot tell the difference.

Much depends, of course, upon the care you take. The first spike of blossoms you have from a new bulb, is due, somebody says, to other care than yours. A bulb makes most of its preparations a year beforehand. But while this is true in a measure, its bloom of next year depends—by the same rule—upon you. Cultivate carelessly and you may well fling away your roots at

the year's end. But if you plant right and
manage right; if when the red and blue
glory of the flowers is departed you give
the green leaves their turn; fostering them
with no less care, and giving them every
facility for perfecting their growth, that the
bulb also may mature and ripen; then you
will have a rich reward for your trouble
and patience. Then you will find (as I have
done) your tulip roots growing larger instead of smaller, from year to year. You
will find none to buy so large, none more
solid. Then, besides the little handful which
you can afford to get new every fall, you
will soon have roots by the basket,—enough
to fill all your spare places, and with some
to bestow upon rooms and gardens more
vacant, perhaps, than yours have ever been.
This is a great pleasure: to place a single
tuft of sweetness in a sick room; to furnish a bright glow of beauty for a room full
of nothing but toil; a spot of freshness for
weary eyes; a reminder of the Lord's good
hand for hearts bowed down with sadness.

No one knows but those who have been too poor to buy one hyacinth, what even one hyacinth can do.

Therefore, for every reason, take the best care of your bulbs. Save even the little off-sets. Well planted and cared for, they will make fine flowering roots in a year cr two, and may yield a good deal even before that. I have got much pleasure from them in this way: If mixed in among the full grown bulbs, they would look insignificant; therefore I plant them by themselves, as they come, with not much arranging, but in good soil and at proper distances. And they make a sort of small world by themselves. Little spikes and little bulbs, but the clearest, fairest colours; not looking much like hyacinths, nor much like anything else, unless a fairy garden. Planted so, you may fill a bed with them, or let them be one of the features in a large bed,—a lovely little variety, a cluster of baby blooms. Or they will make a pretty edging to a border. Only give them all care, treat them

with all respect, and they will pay you
well.

There are many common garden bulbs
and tubers, quite hardy, that may be left un-
stirred from year to year — indeed do best
so. The daffodil, of blessed childhood memory, with the *Poet's narcissus* and *Orange
Phonis* of the same family, and *Double
White* and *Incomparable.* Then there are
peonies — great masses of colour or of whiteness; and dicentra; and amaryllis longi-
flora, a very fine hardy bulb. In fact, *I*
always want every thing I can get! — and
some that I can not.

DECEMBER.

These naked shoots,
Barren as lances, among which the wind
Makes wintry music, sighing as it goes,
Shall put their graceful foliage on again,
And more aspiring, and with ampler spread,
Shall boast new charms, and more than they have
lost.
                                                    —Cowper.

IT is one of the happy things in this fitful
human life, that we are all so ready to
bridge over the times and places that seem
empty and without interest. Once let the
present lose relish, and straightway we
stretch out our hands to grasp the future,
and taste its sweets by anticipation. So
extremes meet, and the echo of departing
wheels gives place to the faint roll of the
approaching, and the days of loss pass
gently on into days of hope.

Winter days are not often called by that

name; yet they are days of patient waiting,
" and if we hope for that we see not, then
do we with patience wait for it."

Patient waiting,—yes, that is it. I had
left my garden in the bright, brave glory
of November; I came back to find it con-
quered, frost-bound, white with December's
snow. Not a bud, not a blossom; not even
the cheery face of one of my pansies to welcome me home. Where are they all?
Waiting. Even so must I wait, yet not in
uncertainty. For "while the earth re-
maineth, seed-time and harvest, and cold
and heat, and summer and winter, and day
and night, shall not cease." I know that
the shrivelled leaves will have fair, fresh,
successors. I know that hid away in the
deep brown earth my tulips and hyacinths
are safe; perfecting their roots, preparing
for a glorious blooming by and by.

All tender things that need protection
should have it before the ground freezes to
any depth; yet put it on as late as possible.
The bulb beds need five or six inches of

dry leaves, if you can get them ; if not, use litter or straw or some such substitute. Spread the leaves smoothly, and keep in place with a layer of light brush. Tender roses may be pegged down and sheltered with an arched roof of sods; or common earth will answer nearly as well, unless the soil be stiff and full of clay. I think many dwarf kinds keep better if they are pruned close before covering; but it is easy to protect the whole bush if you open a slight trench at one side, and fasten the branches down in that. If the bush is too tall to lay down, a cone of straw or cedar brush will protect it well.

Hardy perennials — pinks, chrysanthemums, lilies, and such like, will repay the trouble of covering them too; but a very slight dressing of litter or leaves is quite enough.

The garden will look pretty then, in its winter dress, when all this is done; and under their double blanket of leaves and snow, the roses and lilies will bide their time, and your bulbs wait safely for the spring.

It is less easy to take care of the indoor treasures,—they are so easily killed with kindness. Of course they must be kept from frost; and a few tender ones, such as coleus and achyranthus, like a really warm room. But most common plants winter best in a dreamy state of inaction, unless they can have the regulated heat and moist air of a greenhouse. Put geraniums and fuchsias and roses and even lantanas, in a frost-proof room or cellar, giving them little water if they have little light, and they will "worry through" the winter somehow, and come out all ready for pruning and planting in the spring. If you have more *zonale* geraniums than you know what to do with, set them close together in an old box, packing it quite full, and then fill in between with earth. Or you may hang them up in your cellar, heads down, with no earth within sight, and they will contrive to live along even so.

Examine all your house bulbs from time to time; and when the long roots come near the bottom of the glasses, and the bulbs in pots begin to get an impatient look about the tips of their green or white shoots, as if they meant to rise in the world whether or no, then bring them into a warm room and the fullest light you can give. A few at a time is the pleasantest way, that so each may be enjoyed with the completest enjoyment, taking first those that seem the most forward. Place them as near as possible to your sunniest window; and remember that *now* they will be very thirsty things indeed. Yet do not turn the soil into mud. I have not forgotten yet the look of one poor beauty, which seemed to have been just drowned out. The owner shewed it, exulting; but the tender green shoot got no further.

Turn the pots often, after they are placed in the window, to keep the plant-growth erect and symmetrical. It is melancholy enough to see a tall hyacinth lopping all to one side in its eagerness to find the sun ; not rising proudly up from its encircling leaves, but creeping out between them towards the window. Keep watch, therefore, and straighten your plants (of all sorts) every day if need be, by turning them round. The mere flower stem, of course, you could tie up ; but the bells would still have their own way. And besides, things never look so pretty tied, if they will stand up without it.

Sometimes the leaves seem to get ahead of the flowers, and they grow tall and strong, while the little head of blossoms peeps timidly out from the very bottom of the cluster, but ventures no more. If you see this weakness of disposition in any of your hyacinths, then treat them thus : Twist up a small cone of rather thick paper, leaving a little hole at the small end, and set it down close over the blossom shoot, within the leaves. Thrown thus into sudden twilight, with a single spot of brilliant light above its head, the spike will generally soon tire of its seclusion and begin to grow; stretching itself up, reaching towards the sunshine which comes glinting through the paper cone and tells of the wonderful world beyond. And once in fair progress, the cone may be taken off and the aroused shoot left to itself.

Bulbs in the house are much more likely to suffer from heat than cold. This is true of almost all house plants. Yet some few like the heat; and it now and then happens that a young seedling, or delicate just-rooted cutting, gets chilled. A keen wind sifting in through the window, a sudden change of weather, a neglected fire, may bring this about; and then the little plant droops and hangs its head, and looks unmistakably forlorn. In such cases I have found nothing so good as setting the plant at once in a very warm place. Sometimes on a high shelf in a stove-heated room, sometimes on the hearth before our open wood fire, I have placed the chilled things; and presently, leaf by leaf, they would re-

vive and straighten up and "come to.'
Of course you must watch carefully against
their getting *too* hot.

But if the plants have been not only
chilled but frozen, then you must treat them
just the other way. Keep them as cool as
possible (only above more freezing), and let
neither fire nor sun come near them. A
cold shower-bath will be much more bene-
ficial.

Do they say that last words should be
few? There are so many words that might
be said about flowers, which even with all
my talking I have failed to speak!

For instance, you all want to find out the
secret of perpetual violets, which—(honest-
ly) I do not know myself. "Ever-blooming"
varieties are in the catalogues, but whether
they will really give twelve months of
sweetness—or six, for that matter—in return
for anything less expensive than glass and
gardeners, is something I have never yet
proved to my own satisfaction. Even
violets have their notions. It used to be

said in New York, that the double Neapolitans would not bloom south of Twentieth street for love or money.

Then winter roses. If you can keep a set of them in pots through the summer, or even from the early fall, giving them the best of ca.e and attention, so that the pots will be full of *working roots*, *i. e.*, the little white, tender rootlets which are the very power of a *working* plant; and if you can give the roses abundant moisture overhead, and 50° by night and 65°–70° by day,—and if you have the right kinds,—then you may have plenty of bloom all winter.

If this is not possible for you, as it rarely is for me, then be content with substitutes. Take forget-me-nots, when the violets fail; and when those pass away, enjoy the beauty of your blue lobelias. And for the roses,— you must learn to love even the leafless twigs, and to wait. Bulbs will give you colour, and sedums will give you soft green to contrast with your darker ivy; and Solanum jasminoides will climb over your windows and cover itself, the winter through, with lovely white clusters of bloom.

> "There are briars besetting every path
>   That call for patient care ;
> There is a cross in every lot,
>   And an earnest need for prayer ;
> But a lowly heart that leans on Thee,
>   Is happy anywhere."